Lyndon B. Johnson School of Public Affairs
Policy Research Project Report
Number 64

Federal Regulatory Reform Programs and the Use of Cost-Benefit Analysis

A report by the
Policy Research Project on Federal Regulatory Impact Analysis
The University of Texas at Austin
1984

Library of Congress Card Number: 84-82015
ISBN: 0-89940-666-1

Printed in the U.S.A.

POLICY RESEARCH PROJECT PARTICIPANTS

John M. Berghammer, B.A. (Math), Saint Mary's University, San Antonio, Texas

Michele A. Dunkerley, B.A. (Economics), Skidmore College, Saratoga Springs, New York

Karen P. Greider, B.A. (Political Science), Grinnell College, Grinnell, Iowa

Myriam L. LeMay, B.A. (History), University of Florida, Gainesville, Florida

Brian A. Leugs, B.A. (Economics), Kalamazoo College, Kalamazoo, Michigan

Rita E. Percival, B.A. (English), University of Texas, Austin, Texas

G. Michelle Scott, B.A. (Government), Abilene Christian University, Abilene, Texas

Sabrina F. Strawn, B.A. (Economics/Political Science), Trinity University, San Antonio, Texas

<u>Project Director</u>

Leigh B. Boske, Ph.D.
Associate Professor
Lyndon B. Johnson School of Public Affairs

TABLE OF CONTENTS

Page

FOREWORD.......... ix

EXECUTIVE SUMMARY.......... xi

CHAPTER 1: Regulation and Regulatory Reform.......... 1

Introduction.......... 1
Evolution of the Regulatory Reform Movement.......... 1
Substantive and Procedural Approaches to Regulatory Reform.......... 6
Substantive and Procedural Reform in the Three Branches.......... 10

CHAPTER 2: Recent Executive Regulatory Relief Programs.......... 17

Ford: Executive Order 11821.......... 17
Carter: Executive Order 12044.......... 18
Reagan: Executive Order 12291.......... 19
Conclusion.......... 29

CHAPTER 3: An Evaluation of the RIAs Performed in the Reagan Administration.......... 31

Introduction.......... 31
Cost-Benefit Analysis and Its Components.......... 31
Conformance of the RIAs with OMB Guidance.......... 36
Conformance with Cost-Benefit Standards.......... 39
Conclusion.......... 46

CHAPTER 4: Refinements to the Regulatory Process.......... 49

Introduction.......... 49
The Process Redefined.......... 49
Alternative Analytical Frameworks.......... 57
Conclusion.......... 60

APPENDIX 1: Text of Executive Order 12291.......... 63

APPENDIX 2: DOT Checklist for RIAs.......... 69

APPENDIX 3: History of Cost-Benefit Analysis by the Federal Government.......... 71

END NOTES.......... 75

LIST OF FIGURES

Page

Figure 1: Major Regulatory Bodies of the U.S. Government........ 3

Figure 2: Functions and Procedures of Federal Regulatory and Rulemaking Bodies.............................. 8

Figure 3: Current and Potential Control over Regulatory Bodies by the Three Branches of Government.......... 11

Figure 4: Significant Provisions of S 1080 as They Would Amend the Administrative Procedures Act............. 13

Figure 5: OMS's Requirements for a Satisfactory RIA............ 23

Figure 6: The Proposed System, Phase One: Announcement and Classification................................... 51

Figure 7: The Proposed System, Phase Two: Analysis and Comment.. 55

TABLE

Table 1: Disposition of Regulations Reviewed Under E.O. 12291... 28

Foreword

The Lyndon B. Johnson School of Public Affairs has established interdisciplinary research on policy problems as the core of its educational program. A major part of this program is the nine-month policy research project, in the course of which two or three faculty members from different disciplines direct the research of ten to twenty graduate students of diverse backgrounds on a policy issue of concern to a government agency. This "client orientation" brings the students face to face with administrators, legislators, and other officials active in the policy process, and demonstrates that research in a policy environment demands special talents. It also illuminates the occasional difficulties of relating research findings to the world of political realities.

This report on the use of cost-benefit analysis in the evaluation of federal regulation under the Reagan Administration is the product of a policy research project conducted at the LBJ School in the 1982-83 academic year by Professor Leigh B. Boske and eight graduate students. It was edited and revised in the summer of 1984 by Professor Boske and Brian Leugs. Funding for publication was provided by the Lyndon B. Johnson Foundation.

The curriculum of the LBJ School is intended not only to develop effective public servants but also to produce research that will enlighten and inform those already engaged in the policy process. The project that resulted in this report has helped to accomplish the first task; it is our hope and expectation that the report itself will contribute to the second.

Finally, it should be noted that neither the LBJ School nor The University of Texas at Austin necessarily endorses the views or findings of this study.

Max Sherman
Dean

EXECUTIVE SUMMARY

Federal regulatory reform has been a primary concern in the last three administrations. Presidents Ford, Carter, and Reagan issued executive orders implementing their reform programs. These have had two common elements. First, each required an analysis of the economic impact of new "major" regulations. Second, each authorized a central body to oversee the review of these regulations.

Valuable lessons are learned from experience and there is no reason why mistakes must be repeated in future regulatory reform programs. After summarizing prior executive and congressional reform efforts and judicial developments, this study focuses on the latest reform system, embodied in President Reagan's Executive Order 12291. The weaknesses discovered in this President's program clearly suggest the need for a better method of regulatory reform and oversight. Therefore, this report, the result of a Policy Research Project at the LBJ School of Public Affairs at the University of Texas at Austin, should be useful to future policymakers as the search for an effective and fair regulatory process continues.

SUMMARY OF FINDINGS

Executive Order 12291 required an executive agency having regulatory responsibilities to prepare a Regulatory Impact Analysis (RIA) when proposing major regulations and rules. Independent regulatory agencies and commissions were requested to do the same. An RIA would meet the requirements of the Executive Order if it could document that

1. there is adequate information concerning the need for and consequences of the proposed action;

2. the potential benefits to society outweigh the potential costs; and,

3. of all the alternative approaches to the given regulatory objective, the proposed action will maximize net benefits to society.

The agency was directed to use cost-benefit analysis (CBA) to meet the last two requirements.

The policy research project uncovered three basic problems with this approach. First, the Office of Management and Budget (OMB), in its oversight role, had far too much discretion and too little accountability. Section 6(a)(4) of the Executive Order gave OMB the right to grant waivers to the RIA requirement or regulatory review requirement for any proposed or existing major rule subject to the oversight of the President's Task Force on Regulatory Relief. The Task Force, though, spent its resources on the review of existing regulations. There were no criteria (at least publically acknowledged) for the OMB waiver. Second, OMB failed to provide the guidance necessary to ensure consistently useful reports.

Most important, though, the use of cost-benefit analysis as a justification for regulatory action or inaction implies that this type of analysis is scientifically objective. It became obvious, however, that political decisions were being made under the guise of an objective framework. Every President has a right to be political. However, the decisions should be acknowledged as such.

The system proposed in Chapter 4 corrects these defects by, first, stating that no regulatory decision should be based solely on the result of quantitative analysis. Analysis will still be required but quantification will not be abused and alternatives to a cost-benefit framework will be required in certain instances. The final decision may well be based on these studies but responsibilities will lie with people. Second, there is a well-defined procedure for proposing and promulgating regulatory changes, based on the current Administrative Procedures Act (APA), and suggestions on how to determine the type of analysis to use. This system will not be subverted through informal, undocumented waivers or agreements. The proposed system increases accountability for decisions, correctly placing them in the political arena.

OUTLINE OF THE REPORT

Chapter 1 will give the reader the broad perspective that is necessary for a critical appraisal of the President's efforts and alternative approaches to regulatory reform. It will present several of the facets of regulation that make it such a complex area to reform. The distinction between economic and social regulation is crucial as is the distinction between the regulatory roles of the three branches of government.

Chapter 2 begins with a focus on the regulatory reform programs of Presidents Ford and Carter. The balance of the chapter is devoted to President Reagan's program--in theory and practice. OMB actions (waivers) and inaction (failure to issue detailed guidelines) undermined the system, although several agencies conducted excellent analyses. For example, the Department of Transportation (DOT) and the Environmental Protection Agency (EPA) RIAs were above average. Both wrote in-house guidelines for their analysts. These are also reviewed in the chapter.

Cost-benefit analysis is a well-defined technique and Chapter 3 describes the "state-of-the-art" in this field. An evaluation of the early RIAs, from 1981 and 1982, follows. They will be adjudged by their conformity with the OMB standards and generally-accepted CBA principles. The government analyses vary considerably in quality but, in general, are not satisfactory.

Chapter 4 has two parts. The first outlines in considerable detail a proposed refinement of the Administrative Procedures Act. The process retains much of the existing framework and introduces new elements, such as a Regulatory Advisory Board. Several critical objectives are fulfilled: the regulatory process is unified and simplified and greater public awareness of proposed regulatory action is generated.

The analysis required in this proposed system should be of one of three types. The second half of the chapter describes the three types of analysis--cost-benefit analysis, cost-effectiveness analysis, and multiobjective analysis. All move away from the emphasis on quantification prescribed by OMB (although quantification is required where possible). The choice of which type of analysis to use is, of course, left to the discretion of the agency, but guidelines for the appropriate choice are suggested. These are based on the specificity of and budgetary restrictions in the enabling legislation.

In conclusion, there are five general principles that must be followed in an effective regulatory review process. First, while political considerations cannot be excluded from the regulatory process, the process itself must bring these into the open as much as possible. Decisions should not be hidden behind supposedly objective criteria. However, *ex parte* activities should be explicitly prohibited. Second, analysts must recognize that there is not a single analytical method which is universally applicable to all regulatory situations. Clearly written and comprehensive guidelines must be provided which will offer means to decide which type is the most appropriate. These must also explicitly set forth the way in which the chosen method is applied. Third, the process of rulemaking should be open to public participation as much as possible. Fourth, the development of a written case record should begin early in the process. Finally, while the process for most regulations should take a minimum of time, there must be provisions that will guarantee that the exceptional case, one of a more complex or controversial nature, will receive the maximum amount of consideration.

Members of this project have a strong commitment to efficient and rational regulation. Yet, they also recognize the political environment in which regulations are created and carried out. The regulatory development system must be flexible enough to encompass political realities. This, however, must be balanced by safeguards so that the system cannot be abused or bypassed. This is what the regulatory reform debate boils down to and we believe this proposal, in practice, would pass the test.

CHAPTER 1
REGULATION AND REGULATORY REFORM

INTRODUCTION

This chapter will introduce the facets of regulation and regulatory reform that must be understood before regulatory reform can be analyzed. It will present three concepts: the evolution of regulatory activity and reform (making the critical distinction between economic and social regulation); the regulatory procedure and the difference between substantive and procedural regulatory reform; and, finally, the roles, responsibilities, and activities of the three branches of the federal government in regulatory reform.

EVOLUTION OF THE REGULATORY REFORM MOVEMENT

Adam Smith's treatise on capitalism and laissez-faire economics, An Inquiry into the Nature and Causes of the Wealth of Nations, was published in 1776. The evolving United States of America took many of Smith's principles to heart, including that of free and unrestricted markets. With few exceptions, the government did not intervene in the private sector. Soon, though, imperfections in the operation of the market began to appear. This was the case in the late nineteenth century when railroads were perceived as having too strong a grip on the commerce of the nation. The populist mood in the country forced the federal government to intervene in the private sector through the establishment of the Interstate Commerce Commission (ICC) and the enactment of antitrust laws.

Government intervention in the market via regulation grew at an accelerated pace in the wake of the Great Depression of the 1930s. Congress created additional agencies and commissions to regulate the airline, trucking, telecommunications, and financial securities industries. However, by the late 1960s and early 1970s, there was a radical change in the character of regulations that began to appear. The objective of these new regulations was to incorporate the social costs of various market failures and externalities into the private market's pricing mechanism. The regulations focused on issues of health, safety, environment, and equity. They encompassed the conditions under which goods and services were produced, their impacts on people and the environment, and the physical characteristics of manufactured products. This type of regulation came to be known as "social regulation." It ranges from national ambient air quality standards and consumer product labeling requirements to detailed safety specifications regarding industrial machinery.

Ashford makes a critical distinction between economic regulation and regulation for health, safety, and environmental protection. Economic regulation results in lower prices for the regulated goods by ensuring that the market is competitive and allocates goods efficiently. Health, safety, and environmental regulations, on the other hand, will inevitably result in higher prices since they try to bring the social costs associated with the production and distribution of the regulated goods or industry into the pricing mechanism.[1]

The impact of social regulation was much wider than that of traditional economic regulation. Social regulation cut a wide swathe across all business and industry. For example, whereas the Interstate Commerce Commission (ICC) was established in 1887 to regulate only the transportation sector, the Occupational Safety and Health Administration (OSHA), established in 1970, is responsible for work conditions in many industries--from railroads to petrochemicals. Even the responsibilities of many of the older agencies and commissions were enlarged to encompass goals related to health, safety, and a clean environment.

The change in the character and objectives of regulation is apparent in Figure 1, a list of major economic and social regulatory bodies.[2] This list illustrates the extent of the growth and directional change in federal regulatory activities. In 1970, there were eight economic regulatory agencies and twelve social regulatory agencies. By 1975, there were ten of the former and seventeen of the latter. In 1978, when the U.S. Regulatory Council[3] was created by President Carter, there were representatives from twenty executive departments and agencies and eighteen independent agencies.[4]

Social regulation complicated regulatory oversight and analysis. Compared to economic costs, social costs were difficult to identify, define, and quantify. The objectives of this new form of regulation were frequently broad and vague. In a growing economy, experimentation and mistakes in setting social regulations with undetermined impacts might be tolerable. However, when the economy stagnates or slows, this latitude quickly shrinks, and mistakes or miscalculations could have serious consequences.

It is not surprising, then, that the mood for reform and loosening of social regulation is most visible in times of recession, such as 1980 and 1981. The latest round of regulatory reform, Reagan's approach, is a result of economic conditions as well as political ideology. Indeed, the Reagan Administration considered regulatory reform to be one of the three pillars of its economic recovery plan, along with tax reduction and budgetary spending cuts.[5] The Administration's initial efforts were followed by the Congress shortly thereafter.

There has been no lack of criticism regarding the growing regulatory role of the government. Those being regulated have criticized the restrictiveness and economic costs of many of the regulations. Some claim that regulation, in many instances, has been counterproductive or carried out inefficiently. Some within the government have criticized these trends as well.

Just as the United States, in a mood of pragmatism, cast aside strict observance of the principle of a totally unrestricted private marketplace when its shortcomings were revealed, so now it has embarked on a critical reappraisal of the substance of regulation and the procedures that have evolved over the years. The regulatory reform movement gained momentum from the oil embargo by the Organization of Petroleum Exporting Countries (OPEC) in 1973. The emergence of "stagflation"--the simultaneous existence of unacceptably high rates of inflation and unemployment--in the 1970s was magnified by OPEC's quadrupling of oil prices. The need for a reappraisal of traditional regulatory frameworks and processes became evident when it became widely accepted that unnecessary regulation contributes to stagflation.

Figure 1

Major Regulatory Bodies of the U.S. Government

Date Created	Title and Location	Responsibility
	ECONOMIC REGULATORY BODIES	
1887	ICC: Interstate Commerce Commission. Independent commission with chairman, vice chairman, plus 10 commissioners.	Regulation of carriers engaged in transportation of interstate commerce (railroads, trucking companies, bus lines, freight forwarders, water carriers, transportation brokers) through entry and exit control, rates and rate structures, etc.
1914	FTC: Federal Trade Commission. Independent administrative agency with chairman plus 3 commissioners.	Regulation of commerce to prohibit unfair methods of competition, unfair or deceptive acts or practices, monopolistic practices (restraint of trade, price fixing, boycotts, illegal combinations, etc.).
1916 approx.	FMC: Federal Maritime Commission. Independent commission with chairman plus 4 commissioners.	Regulation of waterborne foreign and domestic offshore commerce of the U.S. through rates, tariffs, licenses, etc. Reorganized in 1977.
1920/ 1977	FPC/FERC: Federal Power Commission/ Federal Energy Regulatory Commission. Now an independent commission within the Department of Energy. Chairman plus 6 commissioners.	Regulation of the interstate aspects of electric power and natural gas industries, rates or charges for transportation of oil by pipeline by valuation of such pipelines. FPC responsibilities were handed over to newly created FERC in 1977.

Figure 1 (continued)

Date Created	Title and Location	Responsibility
1934	FCC: Federal Communications Commission. Independent agency with chairman plus 6 commissioners.	Regulation of interstate and foreign communications by radio, television, wire, and cable. Entry licensing and some content control.
1934	SEC: Securities and Exchange Commission. Independent agency with chairman plus 4 commissioners.	Regulation to assure investing public of fullest possible disclosure and protection against malpractice in securities and financial markets.
1935	CAB: Civil Aeronautics Board. Independent agency with chairman plus 2 members.	Regulation of civil air transport industry through licensing, rates, fares, etc. Under Airline Deregulation Act of 1978 to be phased out by 1985.
1958	FAA: Federal Aviation Administration. Under Department of Transportation since 1966.	Regulation of civil aviation through control over airports, air traffic controllers, and air navigation.
	SOCIAL REGULATORY BODIES	
1931	FDA: Food and Drug Administration. Under Department of Health and Human Services.	Regulation to prevent impure and unsafe foods, drugs, and cosmetics.
1946/ 1974	AEC/NRC: Atomic Energy Commission/ Nuclear Regulatory Commission. Independent agency with chairman plus 4 commissioners.	Regulation of use of nuclear energy to protect public safety and health and the environment. Licensing, standards setting, inspections, and enforcement.

Figure 1 (continued)

Date Created	Title and Location	Responsibility
1964	EEOC: Equal Employment Opportunity Commission. Independent agency with chairman, vice chairman, plus 3 commissioners.	Prevention of discrimination in all phases of employment under the Civil Rights Act of 1964. Investigation of charges and prosecution of violations.
1970	EPA: Environmental Protection Agency. Quasi-independent agency in the executive branch.	Control and abatement of pollution in areas of air, water, solid waste, noise, radiation, and toxic substances through research, monitoring, standards setting, and enforcement.
1970	NHTSA: National Highway Traffic Safety Administration. Under Department of Transportation.	Regulation through programs on motor vehicle safety, fuel economy, and traffic safety.
1970	OSHA: Occupational Safety and Health Administration. Under Department of Labor.	Regulation of workplace health and safety through standards setting, inspections, enforcement, and prosecution.
1972	CPSC: Consumer Product Safety Commission. Independent agency with chairman plus 4 commissioners.	Regulation of products to prevent undue risk of injury to consumers through research, standards setting, information, and enforcement activities.

Source: U.S. General Services Administration, Office of the Federal Register, The United States Government Manual 1981/82 (Washington, D.C., 1981).

The constituencies for economic and social regulation and deregulation are not what one might expect. President Reagan took a well-publicized stand against excessive, costly, inefficient, and restrictive regulation but found that the business constituency, which so largely accounted for his election, had implicit caveats in its deregulatory beliefs. It wanted relief from the economic costs of <u>social</u> regulation. Under the protection of <u>economic</u> regulation, many businesses and industries had achieved positions that were insulated from true competition.[6] Labor joined with the business sector in expressing qualms about economic deregulation. ICC, for example, recently attempted to extensively deregulate surface freight transportation.[7] Consumer advocate Ralph Nader also called for economic regulatory reform, saying that "our unguided regulatory system undermines competition and entrenches monopoly at the public expense."[8]

To further complicate the regulatory reform scene, many congressional liberals continued to carry on the economic deregulation movement, just as Reagan attempted to back away from it. His Administration, for example, failed to support further deregulation of the trucking industry because the Teamsters Union had vehemently opposed it.

SUBSTANTIVE AND PROCEDURAL APPROACHES TO REGULATORY REFORM

Substantive Regulation and Reform

Substantive reform usually is concerned with only one particular type of regulation or a regulation that is associated with a certain activity, industry, firm, or sector of the economy. Substantive reform may occur in several fashions. First, a regulation that has been created by statute also may be redrawn or abolished by statute. Second, a statute of this type often is given substance by the development, implementation, application, and enforcement of a regulation within the executive branch. The statute may be rendered void of substance if any of these activities do not take place. Finally, if executive inaction is challenged, the courts may become involved in substantive reform. Substantive reform, then, is an issue-by-issue process and focuses on reform after-the-fact.

Regulatory Procedure

Procedural reform is forward looking: it is an attempt to change the process so that "bad" regulations are never promulgated. It is achieved through changes in the process by which regulations are made. The outline of current procedural requirements is embodied in the Administrative Procedures Act (APA), enacted in 1946. The regulations promulgated at that time were comparatively far reaching and complex, and it was felt that a process was needed that defined the authority and responsibilities within the process.[9]

<u>The Brownlow Commission</u>. The Brownlow Commission of the 1930s raised many of the issues that were resolved by the APA. It looked at a possible administrative reorganization of the executive departments, particularly in

terms of the regulatory responsibilities of each. The Commission found that regulatory bodies presented an anomaly in a government divided into three branches. Regulatory bodies were expected to perform executive, legislative, and judicial functions. The problem was how to achieve balance within what the Commission's report called the "headless fourth branch of the government."[10] The Commission recommended that the judicial function within the regulatory body be separated from the executive and legislative functions.

While this recommendation was never adopted, the report served as an impetus for efforts by both the American Bar Association and the federal government that resulted in the creation of the single most important law related to the regulatory responsibilities of the government--the APA. Heretofore, procedural standards had existed throughout the various parts of the executive branch, but they were of mixed quality and their adoption was not guaranteed. The APA contained the standards for all three functions within an agency regarding rulemaking. While the dilemma of effectively balancing the three was never solved, the APA did at least offer some guidance.

<u>The Administrative Procedures Act</u>. Sections 551 and 553 of the APA contain the provisions applying to the creation of most government regulations. Sections 554 and 556, in addition, are followed in many regulations. The procedure outlined in the APA can be called "notice and comment rulemaking." Agencies must give public notice of regulatory plans, allowing the public an opportunity to comment on the proposals.[11] Figure 2 shows how these provisions are carried out by regulatory bodies in their three types of responsibilities--law making (legislative), law deciding (judicial), and law enforcing (executive).

Regulatory bodies participate in three types of rulemaking in carrying out their legislative function: (1) substantive rulemaking--the agency gives substance to statutory mandates that have not explicitly set forth the ways in which a regulatory objective is to be met; (2) interpretive rulemaking--used when the statutory mandate is more explicit but must be applied to a variety of situations that were not specified in the statute; and, (3) procedural rulemaking--used for "housekeeping" issues, those which relate to the day-to-day operating procedures that are followed within the regulatory agency, commission, or department.

It is the activity of substantive rulemaking that has emerged as the most important area for reform. Substantive rulemaking may be carried out by informal, formal, or, increasingly, "hybrid" routes (though this latter alternative is not mentioned in the APA). Each of these areas is described in Figure 2 under the law making function. Informal rulemaking follows the APA. No record of comments or agency hearings is established. Formal rulemaking requires that the final ruling be based on the public comments and hearings records. Hybrid rulemaking also requires that a record or rulemaking file based on comments and hearings be created. Final regulatory decisions must be accountable to this record, which may serve as a justification for the rule in later judicial review.[12]

The choice of which of these routes to follow has become controversial and, at times, has entered the political realm. As the nature of regulatory issues has become more complex, technical, and scientific, the informal

Figure 2

Functions and Procedures of
Federal Regulatory and Rulemaking Bodies

LAW MAKING

Rulemaking: general, looks forward, policymaking, legislative quality.

Classes of Rulemaking

I. SUBSTANTIVE: fills in broadly worded statutes and has the evident power of law.

A. Informal Rulemaking: Most rules are created by this method. No exclusive case record is built.

1. Publish notice of proposed rule in the *Federal Register*.
2. Give opportunity to the public for comments, oral or written. Usually for a 60-day period.
3. Publish final rule in the *Federal Register* with concise statement of its basis and purpose.

B. Formal Rulemaking: Used in a few cases where the enabling statute specifically requires the rule to be based on the record of an agency hearing. Usually used in cases of highly complex, technical, and/or scientific nature.

Procedure approximates that of an adjudicatory hearing (see LAW DECIDING, below).

C. Hybrid Rulemaking: Not mentioned in the Administrative Procedures Act, but courts have encouraged its use for more complex, technical, scientific, and/or controversial issues where the building of a case record is felt to be important. Currently in use by some agencies, such as EPA.

Procedure approximates that of an adjudicatory hearing (see LAW DECIDING, below).

II. INTERPRETIVE: states how agency will interpret statutory mandate. Has practical effectiveness but uncertain legal effect. Has been used at times on controversial issues to avoid public participation. It is informally developed and announced through press statements. On authoritative rulings, interested persons may be given notice and opportunity to comment.

Figure 2 (continued)

III. PROCEDURAL: identifies the organization of the agency, describes methods of operation, lists requirements of practice for rulemaking and adjudicative hearings. While not required, usually regulated persons and interested observers are consulted before implementation.

LAW DECIDING

Adjudicative: specific focus on individual case; sometimes used as a case-by-case approach to policymaking; judicial quality.

Hearing before an administrative law judge or hearing examiner from within the agency; "informal" judicial trial; case record is built.

1. Complaint is brought by agency or an individual party.
2. Questions and answers, cross-examination, objections.
3. Finding of fact and opinion.
4. Final order.
5. May be appealed up through agency and court system.

LAW ENFORCING

Executive: implementation of rules, regulations and statutes rulemaking route has become inadequate. This fact has been recognized by the courts and the agencies handling such issues. When creating regulations that are of this nature, the regulatory body has tended to turn to the formal rulemaking procedure, making certain adjustments to it that have produced the hybrid variety. In some cases, Congress, in enabling legislation, has required this procedure to be used.[13] Because of the importance of procedure in the creation of regulation, procedural reform has become an element of the regulatory reform efforts of all three branches of government.

Procedural Reform

Regulatory procedures must balance efficiency and timeliness with adequate opportunity to incorporate public viewpoints into the record. Procedure also must balance the viewpoints and authority of various actors within government, always acknowledging that final authority rests with the agency. A change in procedure could affect these balances. Proposals for procedural reform have come from all the involved parties. Regulatory reforms to redistribute regulatory authority within the government include the legislative veto, sunset laws, continuous ten-year review of major regulations, regulatory budgets, and increased executive oversight and authority. Proposals to increase public input (also called "democratization" of the regulatory process) include "sunset" requirements (recisions of ineffective and excessively costly programs), greater public input in appointments to federal agencies, subsidies to public interest groups, and the establishment of an Agency for Consumer Advocacy.[14]

SUBSTANTIVE AND PROCEDURAL REFORM IN THE THREE BRANCHES

The theory of balance among the three branches of government becomes real when one examines the control over regulatory bodies that is wielded by the courts, the President, and the Congress (see Figure 3). The remainder of this chapter examines the responsibilities and activities of each in substantive regulatory reform and in the reform of the procedures by which regulations are developed.

Regulatory Reform and the Judiciary

The courts increasingly have been involved in regulatory reform. While the Supreme Court may, by constitutional law, look only at specific issues that are brought to it, its primary influence on regulatory reform has been in procedural matters. The APA is not an inflexible, static embodiment of law. Its applicability has been modified by various court interpretations. Several areas of the regulatory process have received attention from the courts, including the point at which the validity of a final regulation can be challenged; whether judicial review can be made of the procedures and case records used by the agency in formulating a rule; and whether a court can require more public input into the record through hearings (hybrid rulemaking).

Figure 3

Current and Potential Control over
Regulatory Bodies by the Three Branches of Government

EXECUTIVE

1. Appointment and removal of top level officals in the executive departments and agencies. Appointment of commissioners, chairmen, top level officials in the independent agencies.
2. Approval and transmission of budget requests to Congress, control of communications with Congress.
3. Through the Office of Management and Budget, review and oversight of rules and regulations of executive departments and agencies.
4. Issuance of Executive Orders setting procedural requirements in addition to those of the Administrative Procedures Act.
5. Veto of legislation.

LEGISLATIVE

1. Senate: advise and consent on Presidential appointments.
2. House: review of budget requests; setting of budgeting procedures and standards; setting limits on costs to private sector.
3. Substantive: committee hearings; organic, enabling, and deregulation statutes (scope of authorization).
4. Procedural: Administrative Procedures Act of 1946 and amendments.

JUDICIAL

Judicial review:

1. Is the statute constitutional?
2. Does the action follow the statute?
3. Is the action arrived at by fair procedures?
4. Is the action substantively reasonable?

With regard to the first issue, previously any time after a regulation had been implemented, a company could have been charged with a violation, either because of an action taken or not taken. However, within the last decade the courts, in some cases, have required that a challenge to a regulation be resolved before a violation can occur. This change was a judicial recognition that resources can be wasted by complying with a new regulation that eventually may be revised.

Advancing the point at which challenges to a regulation might be entered has caused the courts to face the second issue, the formulation of case records. The use of notice and comment informal rulemaking procedures typically leads to the collection of information that reveals little, if any, of the relevant reasoning behind a given regulatory decision. Substantive case records have been built if formal or hybrid rulemaking procedures are used or if a violation is being appealed before a regulatory body or the courts. Especially in the case of the latter, the courts often have been forced to review cases whose written record of the rulemaking process is inadequate. Because of this, the courts have encouraged the use of hybrid rulemaking procedures.[15]

Finally, the courts, notably the District of Columbia Court of Appeals, are beginning to rule on the regulatory procedure. They have made rulings in specific cases on whether the process was conducted openly and whether the agency was sufficiently informed, through internal and external sources, on the issue.[16]

Regulatory Reform and the Congress

While for many years the Congress concentrated on the creation of specific regulations rather than on regulatory reform, this changed in the mid-1970s. Several congressional subcommittees held hearings on regulatory reform. Proposals for sunset requirements and a consumer advocacy agency appeared during the Ford Administration. There also was substantive reform to deregulate large portions of the airline, trucking, railroad, and banking industries. Legislation for substantive reforms was more prevalent than for procedural reforms until very recently.

Concurrent with the Ford, Carter, and Reagan initiatives to require regulatory analysis, procedural reform attempts by Congress have gained momentum. As a result, in the 96th Congress, there were eight bills similar to the directives of Executive Order (E.O.) 12044. In the 97th Congress, there were eight bills consistent with E.O. 12291, including the Regulatory Reform Act (S 1080).[17] This was the broadest and most significant. A version of it was adopted unanimously by the Senate on March 24, 1982. The bill died when the session closed at the end of the year, but similar bills were introduced in both houses for the 98th Congress. The major provisions of S 1080, as reported by the Senate Judiciary Committee, will be examined next.[18]

S 1080. Figure 4 outlines the significant portions of this version of S 1080. The bill introduces hybrid rulemaking into the APA. As described earlier, this adds a degree of formalization to the informal rulemaking used in the majority of government regulations. It is most helpful in the

Figure 4

Significant Provisions of S 1080 as They Would
Amend the Administrative Procedures Act

1. Tightens up exemptions to APA notice and comment requirements.
   a. Defines "emergency rules." 551(a)
   b. Redefines matters "relating to agency management or personnel." 553(b)(1)(B)
   c. Redefines "interpretive rules and general statement of policy." 553(b)(1)(C)
   d. Redefines "matters related to public property, loans, grants, benefits, or contracts." 553(b)(1)(D)
   e. Redefines rules with "insignificant impact." 553(b)(1)(E)
   f. Exempts "emergency rules." 553(b)(1)(F)

2. Requires documentation of rules exempt under 553(b)(1)(E) and 553(b)(1)(F). 553(b)(2)

3. Requires additional information in notice of proposed rulemaking. Requires that parties be kept apprised of changes in proposed rules and other developments. 553(c)(1)

4. Specifies hybrid rulemaking for major and nonmajor rules. 553(c)(1)
   a. Sixty-day comment period. 553(d)(1)
   b. Opportunity for informal hearings for major rules. 553(d)(2)

5. Requires statement of legal basis and regulatory purpose with the final publication of the rule. 553(e)

6. Requires agency to identify and disclose in the notice of proposed rulemaking the information on which it plans to base the proposed rule. 553(e)(2)

7. Requires that the rulemaking file contain analyses, transcripts of hearings, and "those materials that might reasonably be expected to play an important role during a rulemaking or judicial review of a rule." 553(f)(1)

Figure 4 (continued)

8. Defines "major rule" as
   a. Having $100 million direct or indirect enforcement, compliance, or secondary (market) costs. 621(3)(A)(i)
   b. Anything designated "major" by President or agency. 621(3)(B)

9. Broad definitions of benefits and costs including nonmonetary. 621(4) and 621(5)

10. Preliminary regulatory analysis with the proposed rule including:
    a. Anticipated benefits and costs. 622(c)(i) and 622(c)(2)
    b. Scope of alternatives to include no regulation, alternatives with consideration for regional differences, alternatives with localized enforcement, alternatives using performance and other flexible standards. 622(c)(3)
    c. Explanation of why benefits <u>justify</u> costs or why the chosen alternative is most cost effective. Exception: when enabling statute prohibits cost-benefit consideration. 622(c)(4)

11. Requires final regulatory analysis with final rule. 622(d)
    a. Description and comparison of costs and benefits of the rule and reasonable alternatives quantified where possible. 622(d)(i)
    b. Determine that benefits <u>justify</u> the costs or why the chosen alternative is the most cost effective. Exception: when enabling statute prohibits cost-benefit consideration. 622(d)(2)

12. Makes the decisionmaker accountable for the analyses 622(f)

13. Recognizes the need for flexible executive oversight
    a. Limits on judicial review. For the most part, may not review major/nonmajor classification; may not rule on the analysis itself, only whether agency acted on basis of analysis. 623(a), (b), (c), (d)
    b. Requires executive to establish procedures for evaluating agency compliance. This may be delegated to vice president, but if delegated to anyone else, the person must be confirmed by the Senate. Presidential exercise or nonexercise of this authority

Figure 4 (continued)

not subject to judicial review. 624(a), (b), (c)

14. Review of existing regulations:
    a. Every major rule reviewed every ten years (similar to analysis of new regulations). 631
    b. Biannual regulatory agenda by agencies of rules they expect to propose, promulgate, renew, or withdraw. 632(a)
    c. Judicial review of informal rulemaking. Allow judiciary to independently review whether rule is within the scope of statutory interpretation or if there is substantial support for the rule in rulemaking file. 5(b) of S 1080

Source: U.S. Senate, Committee on the Judiciary, The Regulatory Reform Act, 97th Cong., 1st sess., Senate Report 97-284, to accompany S 1080, pp. 106-175.

examination of regulations that involve highly technical, scientific, and complex data. It also ensures the existence of a case record for judicial review and requires that most relevant executive office comments be included in that record.

Second, the bill recognizes the importance of economic analysis of specific regulations and requires both preliminary and final regulatory impact analyses. In contrast to Reagan's initiative, S 1080 limits the power of the Office of Management and Budget (OMB) to grant waivers and exemptions to the analyses. Benefits are to be compared with costs but instead of requiring benefits to be greater than costs, benefits need only justify costs. This removes the pressure to quantify all impacts and to use cost-benefit analysis as a decision rule.

Third, it calls for strong executive oversight of the process. However, judicial review would ensure that legislative intent is not overridden and that agency decisions are based on the rulemaking file. Finally, S 1080 requires a review, over a ten-year period, of the most important existing regulations. After review, they would be subject to renewal, amendment, or rescission.[19]

Regulatory Reform and the Executive

During the Nixon Administration, regulatory reform was a partisan issue. The recommendations made by his Council of Economic Advisors and the Ash Council did little more than create hostility, although the regulatory reform issue did gain some publicity. However, through the next three administrations, the controversy diminished and Ford, Carter, and Reagan found bilateral support for regulatory reform. This was probably due to economic conditions and public sensitivity to the wide scope of social regulation.[20]

The last three Presidents have issued executive orders outlining procedural changes in the promulgation of regulation. These executive orders imposed no actual constraints on the substance of regulatory decisions; their significance was the procedural requirement that agencies initiate studies of the costs and benefits of proposed regulations and "meaningful alternatives."[21] It was hoped that economic analysis of this type would cause agencies to be more aware of the impacts of their proposed actions. The regulatory relief programs also designated a central body or coalition of executive office staffs to oversee the process and to serve as a clearinghouse for all regulations.

None of these programs made a distinction between the types and purposes of regulations. A case can be made, however, that cost-benefit analysis or economic impact analysis is appropriate only for regulations promulgated under statutes calling for the correction of market failures (e.g., pollution abatement) or efficiency promotion (antitrust). Cost-benefit analysis of regulations promoting distributional goals (e.g., criteria for welfare eligibility) is not logical.[22] The next chapter begins with a description of the efforts of the last three presidents in this two-part approach (oversight and analysis) to regulatory reform.

CHAPTER 2
RECENT EXECUTIVE REGULATORY RELIEF PROGRAMS

FORD: EXECUTIVE ORDER 11821

President Ford introduced his regulatory reform program in a nationally televised speech on October 8, 1974. He called for a National Commission for Regulatory Reform made up of representatives from the Congress, the executive branch, and private interests. It was to "identify and eliminate" existing regulations that increased consumer prices "without any good reason." Second, he directed that major legislative and regulatory proposals "emanating from the executive branch" be accompanied by Inflation Impact Statements (IISs), certifying that "we have carefully weighed the effect on the Nation." Third, the Council on Wage and Price Stability (COWPS) was "to be the watchdog over inflationary costs of all Governmental actions."[23]

This requirement for IISs was put into Executive Order 11821, issued the next month. The Director of OMB was required to develop criteria for designating "major" legislation and rules. In doing this, he was directed to consider their effects on the costs to various groups, on productivity and competition, and on the supply of "important products and services." The Order expired on December 31, 1976, but was renewed by Executive Order 11949. At that time, the analyses were renamed "Economic Impact Statements" (EIIs).[24] Subsequent OMB clarifications called for a description of the costs and benefits of the proposed regulation and alternative strategies.[25]

Ford primarily was concerned with the inflationary effect of unnecessary regulation. Proposed legislation was given to OMB for review, and regulatory proposals were delivered to COWPS.[26] COWPS was required to file comments on the proposals to be included in the regulatory record.[27] It must be noted that the President's preoccupation with the inflationary impact of regulations seemed to ignore the distinction between economic and social regulation. As noted in Chapter 1, the latter is supposed to increase the market price of the regulated good.

Another facet of Ford's program was an interdepartmental study group, called the Domestic Council Review Group on Regulatory Reform. It was composed of OMB, COWPS, Council of Economic Advisors (CEA), Treasury Department, Justice Department, Domestic Council, and other White House personnel. It was directed to prepare specific substantive reforms. Three bills resulted--deregulation of the railroad, motor carrier, and airline industries.[28]

The impact of the IISs was probably minimal. It seems that the analyses were not really incorporated into the decisionmaking process, but, rather, were written to justify regulatory initiatives. Part of the problem may have been that an IIS appeared too late in the promulgation process to affect it. By mid-April of 1977, sixty-five EEIs and IISs had been prepared for proposed regulations and eight for proposed legislation. Most were prepared by a few of the agencies.[29] According to the U.S. Regulatory Council, the IIS requirement was not as successful in "ensuring the regular consideration of the costs of government regulations as President Ford had intended."[30] COWPS and OMB found that implementation was inconsistent, few alternatives were presented in the statements, and "the analyses took place too late in the decision-making process to substantially improve or even affect the outcomes."[31]

CARTER: EXECUTIVE ORDER 12044

President Carter continued his predecessor's substantive and procedural deregulation initiatives. He supported legislation to deregulate the airline, surface transportation, and telecommunications industries. In the area of social regulation, he chose the procedural route, building on Ford's experience.[32]

In March of 1978, President Carter issued Executive Order 12044. This also required regulatory analysis of major proposed rules and a review of existing regulations. The Order was much more specific than Ford's. Major rules were defined as those having an annual impact on the economy of at least $100 million or those that would cause a major increase in prices in certain areas. Extended later in Executive Order 12221, it called for analyses that succinctly stated the problem, described alternatives, analyzed the economic consequences of each alternative, and justified the chosen alternative.[33]

Rules were not subjected to cost-benefit tests, but agencies were to identify costs and benefits, quantify them to the extent possible, and choose the most cost-effective solution. Notice of proposed rulemaking was to include an explanation of the regulatory approach, a description of alternatives considered, and information on how to receive a copy of the draft analysis. Agencies were to prepare an evaluation plan to monitor the effects of the new regulation.[34]

A considerable amount of discretion was left to the agency. In their internal procedures, agencies were directed to publish a "semiannual agenda of regulations." Agency heads were to classify regulations as "significant," based on the number of people affected, compliance costs, effects on competition, and relationship to other regulations in the same area. Public comment on these regulations was to be open for at least sixty days and each significant regulation had to be approved at the preliminary and final stages by the agency head.[35]

Agencies also were asked to periodically review their existing regulations. The decision to review was to be based on general factors such as the number of complaints received, duplication of regulations, the general "regulatory burden" that accompanied it, and the length of time since the regulation had been reviewed.[36]

Carter's program for executive oversight also was broader than Ford's. The task of implementing and overseeing the program fell on a loose coalition of staff offices within the executive office. A new group was established--the Regulatory Analysis Review Group (RARG)--chaired by the CEA and consisting of representatives from the regulatory departments and the executive office. RARG and COWPS, in general, reviewed the proposals and analyses.[37]

RARG could be considered a peer review body. Each year it reviewed between ten and twenty of the costliest proposed regulations. The CEA and COWPS provided staff support for the preparation of RARG reports. These reports reviewed the analyses written by agencies for their major rules. Drafts of RARG reports were written by CEA and COWPS analysts and were circulated to all RARG members, as well as to the agency whose proposal was under review. After this, the group formally discussed the particular issue. Comments and dissents were incorporated into the draft and a final report was placed in the public record at the close of the comment period. The reports ensured that White House concerns were a part of the rulemaking record.[38]

In short, under Carter there was ample chance for public and executive office comment on regulatory proposals. Regulatory analysis was required at two stages in the process--with the publication of the proposed rule and the final rule. This meant that analysis would enter the picture earlier in the decisionmaking process. Finally, oversight was expanded and decentralized.

REAGAN: EXECUTIVE ORDER 12291

Context of The Order

President Reagan strengthened the process of regulatory oversight. On January 22, 1981, his second day in office, he created the cabinet-level Task Force on Regulatory Relief. The Task Force, later formalized in the Executive Order, is chaired by Vice President Bush and includes Treasury Secretary Regan, Attorney General Smith, Commerce Secretary Baldridge, Labor Secretary Donovan, OMB Director Stockman, Assistant to the President for Policy Development Anderson, and Council of Economic Advisors Chairman Weidenbaum. The Executive Director of the Task Force initially was James C. Miller III, of the Office of Information and Regulatory Affairs (OIRA) in OMB. OMB also provides the staff support for the Task Force.[39] The Task Force is directed to review pending regulations, study existing regulations for revision, and recommend legislative proposals for both substantive and procedural reform.[40]

One week after creating the Task Force, Reagan postponed pending regulations--those that were scheduled to become effective within the next sixty days that had been issued at the close of the Carter Administration. He also asked agencies to refrain from proposing new rules for the next sixty days. This was to ensure that the "midnight rules" from the previous Administration were cost effective, to allow the presidential appointees to become comfortable in their positions, and to allow the Administration to develop its own regulatory oversight procedure.[41]

Executive Order 12291

The final word in President Reagan's regulatory reform package was contained in Executive Order 12291, issued February 17, 1981. Appendix 1 contains the text of the Order. Each agency is required to prepare a Regulatory Impact Analysis (RIA) for every major rule (with several exceptions). Major is defined as a rule "that is likely to result in" the following:

1. an effect on the economy of $100 million or more annually;

2. significant adverse effects on prices for consumers, individual industries, government agencies, or geographic regions; or,

3. significant adverse effects on "competition, employment, investment, productivity, innovation," or the international competitiveness of U.S. exporters.[42]

The Director of OMB has the authority to declare any rule to be major.[43] The Director also can waive the requirements for a major rule.[44]

Moreover, the Director is responsible for filling in the details of the reform and review program. In the Order, he is directed to "prepare and promulgate uniform standards for the identification of major rules and the development of RIAs"[45] and to "develop procedures for estimating the annual benefits and costs of agency regulations, on both an aggregate and economic or industrial sector basis, for purposes of compiling a regulatory budget."[46]

The RIA must contain

1. a description of the potential benefits of the rule, including any beneficial effects that cannot be quantified in monetary terms, and the identification of those likely to receive the benefits;

2. a description of the potential costs of the rule, including any adverse effects that cannot be quantified in monetary terms, and the identification of those likely to bear the costs;

3. a determination of the potential net benefits of the rule, including an evaluation of effects that cannot be quantified in monetary terms;

4. a description of alternative approaches that could substantially achieve the same regulatory goal at lower costs, together with an analysis of this potential benefit and costs (sic) and a brief explanation of the legal reasons why such alternatives, if proposed, could not be adopted; and,

5. if necessary and not covered under number four, an explanation of the legal reasons why the rule cannot be evaluated on the basis of costs and benefits.[47]

Two features of the review process for new regulations should be noted. First, and most important, OMB and its Director have an incredible amount of discretion. He can waive the process; section 8(b) states that "the Director [of OMB], subject to the direction of the Task Force, may, in accordance with the purpose of this Order, exempt any class or category of regulations from any or all requirements of this Order."[48] The Director not only is called on to establish criteria for determining if a proposed regulation is major, but he can also determine which rules fit this category. Furthermore, he can delay the process. If he notifies the agency that he intends to submit comments for the record or if he requests a consultation, he can postpone the process. The clock can be stopped, as it were, because agencies are not to publish preliminary or final RIAs or notices until the Director's comments are received and addressed.[49]

Miller was well aware of OMB's power in this area. In an interview with Regulation magazine, he explained:

> Actually, the OMB can identify a rule as major, and thus bring it into the review and consultation process, for reasons some may regard as wholly without merit. The $100 million definition of major rule is for the guidance of the agencies, not the OMB. There is no limit on what OMB can designate as major.[50]

In addition, there seems to be no limit on what OMB can exempt from being classified as major. When asked if, when a regulation that had an $800 million impact on the economy was revised, reducing the impact to $200 million, it must go through the RIA process, Miller answered, "If OMB, again under task force direction, were convinced on the basis of evidence, however sparse, that such a reduction would occur, a waiver would be granted immediately."[51] This indicates that waivers can be granted by the OMB to support deregulation, without considering the benefits of the original regulation and, therefore, the implicit costs of the deregulation.

There are other significant provisions in the Order. There is to be considerable consultation between the agency and OMB before notices of proposed rulemaking and final rules are published.[52] Second, section 5 requires each agency to publish biannually a regulatory agenda of proposed regulations that it "has issued or expects to issue" and the status of regulations undergoing review in the process. The regulations must be summarized and the objectives, legal basis, and schedule for action must be included in the report.[53] Third, an internal review process is prescribed for the agency. Agencies must determine that a rule is within their legal authority and that "the factual conclusions upon which the rule is based have substantial support in the agency record, viewed as a whole, with full attention to public comments in general and the comments of persons directly affected by the rule."[54] Fourth, OMB is to act as a clearinghouse to "identify duplicative, overlapping and conflicting rules...[and, if necessary,] require appropriate interagency consultation to eliminate such duplication, overlap, or conflict."[55]

The Executive Order outlines the review procedure for pending regulations and distinguishes between rules which have been promulgated but have not yet become effective and those which have been prepared but not promulgated. The most striking feature is the potential for OMB to delay the regulatory process, even as the regulation is being developed and presented.

Early Results

By the time Executive Order 12291 was in effect, the Department of Education had withdrawn the bilingual education rules; the Department of Energy (DOE) had rescinded several energy conservation measures; the Department of Transportation (DOT) had delayed passive restraint rules; and Reagan himself revoked Executive Order 12265, which dealt with reporting requirements for exporting some hazardous substances.[56]

On March 25, just before the sixty-day freeze was lifted, Vice President Bush released a list of thirty-five "midnight regulations" that were to be postponed,[57] as well as a list of twenty-seven existing regulations that were to be reviewed.[58] He also announced that he had sent letters to

1. heads of executive agencies informing them of the abolition of the Regulatory Council;
2. heads of independent agencies asking for their cooperation in following the procedures and spirit of Executive Order 12291; and,
3. about one hundred "labor organizations, businesses, trade associations, State and local governments, and academic groups," requesting advice on areas for substantive regulatory reform.[59]

According to the General Accounting Office, of the seventeen independent agencies that were requested to voluntarily comply with the Executive Order, "several" promised to comply "to the fullest extent possible." In general, the agencies were reluctant to become involved with OMB during the promulgation process. Only the Civil Aeronautics Board (CAB) agreed to discuss possible regulations with OMB prior to publication. Most agencies felt that their internal review processes were sufficient.[60]

Subsequent OMB Guidelines

On June 13, 1981, OMB issued interim guidelines for preparing RIAs. The language indicates that the RIAs are to serve as a tool for evaluators to use to ascertain if "the ojectives of E.O. 12291 were met." The guidelines call for a wide range of alternatives, ranging from "no regulation" and "market-oriented" options to alternatives "beyond the scope" of the enabling legislation. Quantification of benefits and costs is required if they "[can] be estimated." However, the system seems to require that the decision be based on maximizing social benefits. Thus, while quantification is not mandated in all cases, it appears that decisions are to be based on quantified conclusions.[61] Figure 5 gives a concise outline of OMB's interim guidelines.

In its role as an overseer of the review process, OMB probably should have provided more detail in these guidelines. Consistency across departments and agencies in the RIAs required guidance on issues such as how much effort to put into the analyses, how to deal with benefits such as the value of human lives saved, and other economic assumptions and predictions.[62]

Figure 5

OMB'S Requirements for a Satisfactory RIA

1. Statement of need for and consequences of the proposal.
   a. What type of market imperfection needs correction?
   b. How would the proposed regulation correct this?

2. Examination of the alternative approaches to the proposed regulation.
   a. Alternative of "no regulation."
   b. Alternatives outside the scope of the enabling legislation and perhaps outside the jurisdiction of the agency.
   c. Alternatives within the scope of the enabling legislation, including:
      i. Alternative stringency levels;
      ii. Alternative effective dates; and,
      iii. Alternative compliance mechanisms.
   d. Alternative market-oriented approaches, including:
      i. Information on labeling requirements;
      ii. Performance rather than design standards; and,
      iii. Economic incentives.

3. Analysis of benefits and costs
   a. Benefits
      i. Present value of benefits of all alternatives using 10 percent discount rate. Use other discount rates to test sensitivity. Express in constant dollars.
      ii. Describe benefits if nonquantifiable.
      iii. Identify source of data and information and state assumptions.
      iv. Describe mechanism by which benefits will occur.
      v. Identify the <u>type</u>, <u>recipient</u>, and <u>timing</u> of benefit.
   b. Costs
      i. Present value of costs of all alternatives using 10 percent discount rate. Use other discount rates to test sensitivity. Express in constant dollars.
      ii. Describe costs if nonquantifiable.
      iii. Identify source of data and information and state assumptions.

Figure 5 (continued)

iv. Identify the type, bearer, and timing of costs.

v. Identify adverse effects of regulation (e.g., reduce productivity, discourage innovation, reduce competition).

vi. Identify transfer payments and significant increases in costs to government levels.

c. Estimate net benefits by subtracting costs from benefits for each alternative.

i. Identify nonmonetary and nonquantifiable benefits and costs.

ii. Use sensitivity analysis when assumptions are uncertain.

iii. Where many benefits are not quantifiable, present alternatives to show cost effectiveness of each.

4. Rationale for choosing proposed regulatory action.

a. Ordinarily based on greatest net benefits.

b. If legal constraints prohibit this, describe and estimate net cost of these constraints.

5. Cite statutory authority by which agency is authorized to undertake regulatory act.

Source: Executive Office of the President, Office of Management and Budget, "Interim Regulatory Impact Analysis Guidance," Washington, D.C., June 6, 1981.

Agency Guidelines

Individual agencies are free to develop more detailed guidelines applying to the particular mission of the agency and to the types of issues within its regulatory jurisdiction. The Environmental Protection Agency (EPA) and the Department of Transportation (DOT) have chosen to do so. EPA issued a draft of "Guidelines for Performing Regulatory Impact Analyses" on June 22, 1982.[63] These are similar to OMB's instructions but are more detailed due to the very complicated nature of environmental and carcinogenic issues. EPA used the guidelines primarily for evaluating specific regulations controlling individual pollutants.

The EPA guidelines contain an acknowledgement that environmental regulation evaluation is an evolving art and developing guidelines is an ongoing process. The EPA formed an agency-wide group to create specific agency policies regarding the Executive Order. The group circulated many drafts in 1982 for comments, both inside and outside the agency.[64] This project focuses on a June 22 draft.

The June guidelines provide much of the valuable and necessary guidance that OMB failed to specify in the "Interim Guidance" memo. The EPA draft requires that health effects be quantified using the "direct cost [of illness] to the person, including medical costs, loss of work and earnings, and impact on productivity." Analysts are advised to refrain from quantifying the value of human lives saved.[65] Nonhealth benefits are to be quantified based on travel costs (e.g., willingness to travel to enjoy a recreational area) and other "actual market transactions," avoiding surveys of "willingness to pay."[66]

Costs are identified in the draft. These include compliance costs (to the regulated and the regulator), "deadweight welfare loss" (decreases in consumer or producer surplus; see Chapter 4), adjustment costs for displaced resources, and the qualitative impact on "product quality, productivity, innovation, and market structures."[67] Finally, the guidelines acknowledge that the many nonquantifiable impacts and the lack of knowledge regarding carcinogens and disease mechanisms place discretion and accountability with the Administrator.[68]

DOT requires economic analysis of all regulations, not only those designated as major by E.O. 12291. In April of 1982, it issued very comprehensive guidelines in "Guidance for Regulatory Evaluations: A Handbook for DOT Benefit-Cost Analysis."[69] It is similar to OMB's in sequence and content but provides more detail. It includes appendices from outside sources that describe how to calculate costs and benefits, choose discount rates, and assess risk.[70]

DOT recognizes the value of using correct cost-benefit analysis (CBA) techniques:

> There is a standard set of elements or components that are required for any technically proficient cost-benefit analysis. Proper attention to these elements will make the final decision better and

> more defensible in the rule-making process itself and through the required clearance process. It will also allow senior officials and decisionmakers the means of rapidly assessing the rule's implications and assuring them that all important issues have been considered.[71]

There are several interesting points emphasized in the DOT guidelines. First, the level of analysis (effort) must match

1. the level of controversy and public interest;

2. the magnitude and source or burden of costs and benefits;

3. the budget resources available to perform the study; and,

4. the availability and cost of the data.[72]

Second, the guidelines explain why certain steps in the analysis are necessary. Difficult concepts, such as nonquantifiable impacts and the difference between cost-benefit and cost-effectiveness, are illustrated. A cost-benefit summary is presented. Third, it emphasizes that the report should be well organized. Finally, it summarizes the procedure with a checklist to ensure that DOT RIAs are consistent.[73] The checklist is reproduced in Appendix 2.

Procedure in Practice

The major issue in the process in practice is the waiver policy of OMB. In an early study, the General Accounting Office felt that the number of waivers was threatening to undermine the entire program:

> OMB waived the regulatory impact analysis requirement for 21 of the 43 major rules it reviewed in 1982. The rationale for these waivers was often unclear, with the agency giving one reason and OMB giving a different reason or no reason at all. Even where a reason was given (such as sufficient analysis already having been completed), no support was given for this reason (such as a discussion of, or even a citation to, this analysis). We are concerned that so many major rules were allowed to be issued without the benefit of a regulatory impact analysis. We do not believe that agencies are likely to take the value of regulatory impact analyses seriously if the analysis requirement is frequently waived.[74]

As mentioned before, OMB was given a major oversight role in the system so that greater consistency might be achieved. However, consistency in practice has not occurred. OMB's position allows it to act seemingly arbitrarily and informally--quite outside the spirit, but not the letter, of the Executive Order.

In addition to criticizing the waiver policies, the GAO reported that it was concerned about the extent of *ex parte* contacts. "According to OMB officials, OMB discusses pending rules with agency personnel both before and after the rule is sent over for OMB review."[75] In a House subcommittee hearing, Miller was castigated for Task Force communication with private interests. These were seen as an "end-run" around the agencies.[76]

It is likely, however, that the informal consultations noted by GAO led to a more efficient system. Agencies could know early in the process to what OMB would agree. However, this efficiency was at the cost of a loss of accountability, public input, and public awareness. It simply was not clear whether OMB had objective criteria by which to define major rules or grant waivers. Through some unknown process, OMB determined a regulation to be consistent with E.O. 12291 (i.e., with societal benefits greater than societal costs and with societal benefits maximized) or inconsistent. Granted, the Executive Order did allow for exceptions, but it was never clear that the entire system was not based on OMB waivers. If the rule was consistent, OMB could request minor changes or approve it as submitted. If it was classified as inconsistent, the agency could withdraw the rule or revise it. The agency could appeal OMB's decision to the Task Force.

The Results

GAO summarized the results of the regulatory reviews for 1981. This is reproduced in Table 1. In 1981, 2679 new regulations were submitted to OMB for review. Of these, 2446 (91 percent) were approved as submitted; 138 (5 percent) were approved after minor changes, 45 (2 percent) were returned unapproved, and 50 (2 percent) were withdrawn by the agency. Sixty-two of these rules were found to be major: 60 were approved, 1 was returned, and 1 was withdrawn. Only 21 were accompanied by an RIA. As for the 172 frozen rules, 112 (65 percent) were approved; 12 (7 percent) were substantially changed; 18 (10 percent) were withdrawn; and, as of April 1982, 30 (17 percent) were pending. The cumulative effect of OMB action in 1981 was that it caused revisions in 198 (7 percent) regulations and rejected 46 (2 percent).[77]

As for the review of existing regulations, a status report on Task Force activities was released in August of 1982. The Task Force estimated that its review and subsequent revisions "saved" about $6 billion annually and about $10 billion in "one-time investment costs." Fifty-one reforms had been completed and the report announced thirty-five more that would be reviewed. Twenty-five reforms were underway.[78]

Constitutional Issues

The area that has the greatest potential for future problems in this program is the uncertain legality of executive efforts to overturn legislative mandates. However, on careful analysis this seems to be an issue of agency or department independence, rather than a clear violation of the separation of powers. An executive order, by itself, is not a "law." Without

Table 1

Disposition of Regulations Reviewed
by OMB Under E.O. 12291, 1982

	All New Rules		Major New Rules	Frozen Rules	
	Number	Percent		Number	Percent
Approved as submitted	2446	91%		112	65%
Approved after minor changes	138	5%	60		
Approved after substantial amendment				12	7%
Returned unapproved	45	2%	1		
Withdrawn	50	2%	1	18	10%
Still pending				30	17%
Total	2679	100%	62	172	100%

Source: U.S. General Accounting Office, Report to the Chairman, Committee on Governmental Affairs, United States Senate: Improved Quality, Adequate Resources, and Consistent Needed if Regulatory Analysis is to Help Control Costs of Regulations (Washington, D.C., November 2, 1983), pp. 48, 49.

constitutional or statutory authority, therefore, an executive order has no legal effect.[79] Thus, it is possible that an executive department could ignore OMB's procedure and simply follow the APA's requirements for notice and comment. Indeed, some critics have noted that E.O. 12291 could be considered an attempt to amend the APA.[80]

One of the regulations rescinded by the Reagan Administration was the 1977 order for passive restraint systems in new cars. An appeals court found the Administration in violation of procedure on this issue and the Supreme Court was expected to rule on this case in June of 1983. However, this issue seems to boil down to the fact that the President is asking the agencies and departments to follow procedures or to rescind regulations that may be contrary to the intent of the legislation. The regulatory body has ultimate responsibility for its regulations and, thus, is it is accountable to Congress. This being the case, it is the lack of autonomy in the departments that is to blame, not presidential lobbying or influence.

In some instances, enabling legislation may prohibit an agency from using cost and benefit considerations in promulgating a regulation. Executive Order 12291 does not change this prohibition. Indeed, section 2 of the Order only requires cost-benefit analysis "to the extent permitted by law."[81] Granted, this may merely be an obligatory disclaimer.

In addition to the issue of the constitutionality of the President acting as a lawmaker,[82] there is the issue of *ex parte* contacts as a violation of due process. Rosenberg claims that E.O. 12291, in practice, "provides access to the process by government and non-government interests without the safe-guards against secret communication or the exercise of undue influence."[83] The resolution of these constitutional issues could have major implications for this and future executive initiatives to reform regulatory procedures and substance.

CONCLUSION

The Reagan initiative is not very different from the efforts of his immediate predecessors. However, he took an additional step, calling for rigid or "*pure*" cost-benefit analysis (CBA); that is, he implied that decisions were to be based on costs and benefits. Thus, even though OMB was careful to acknowledge that not all impacts could be quantified, decisions were to be to made as if they *could* be quantified. In this way, the Reagan plan went too far and tried to turn subjective regulatory decisions into objective ones. The CBA framework does not take into account distributional issues upon which many regulations are based. Analysis is necessary, but CBA, used in this rigid sense, may not be the correct type. Chapter 4 explains the technique of CBA and shows how the agencies fared in conducting the analyses in conformance with Executive Order 12291.

CHAPTER 3
AN EVALUATION OF THE RIAS PERFORMED IN THE REAGAN ADMINISTRATION

INTRODUCTION

Chapter 2 discussed the Reagan Administration's requirements for cost-benefit analysis (CBA). The agencies have a relatively good framework within which to evaluate their regulations; although the OMB interim guidelines lack detail, its general information is correct. However, compliance with even these general guidelines has been, for whatever reason, minimal in general and not uniform across the departments.

There is another standard by which the RIAs and the OMB guidelines should be adjudged--according to cost-benefit procedures prescribed in academic literature on the subject of CBA. Therefore, this chapter begins with a description of the "state of the art" of CBA. The extent of the shortcomings of the OMB guidance will become clearer, and, not surprisingly, the agency RIAs, almost without exception, will be found lacking as well. The evaluation of specific RIAs, among the first performed by the agencies under the new rule, will end the chapter.

COST-BENEFIT ANALYSIS AND ITS COMPONENTS

Government actions almost certainly have impacts extending beyond the government itself. Sound, rational policy requires the analysis of the potential effects of any contemplated action. Any analytical tool that increases the information available to policymakers should improve decisionmaking. CBA accomplishes this by providing a framework for making comparisons among policy options that quantifies the impacts of those policy options.

In this regard, cost-benefit analysis can be a useful tool, in the event that its inherent limitations are recognized and appropriate steps are taken to make proper adjustments for those limitations. Any attempt, for example, to attach dollar values to all benefits and costs--even when it is inappropriate to do so--typically leads to unreliable results and conclusions. Yet, the Administration wishes to use CBA only in its narrowest sense, alternatively called "monetized cost-benefit analysis"[84] or "formal cost-benefit analysis."[85] Formal CBA requires that an attempt be made to value all benefits and costs in terms of dollars, and program justification rests on total benefits exceeding total costs. Furthermore, Pareto-optimality conditions must be met (at least in theory): one proposed government action is to be preferred over others when one or more persons are made better off and no one else is made worse off.[86]

Informal CBA relaxes these requirements so that benefits and costs not susceptible to quantification may be taken into consideration in other ways; this approach also allows the consideration of distributional effects and transfer payments. No matter what approach is used, however, most experts agree that CBA is no more than a useful tool for decisionmaking.

Moreover, the application of CBA consumes both human and financial resources, which necessitates the establishment of priorities for deciding which particular programs are to be subjected to analysis. Three main criteria can be used. First, the size of the program (or expected impacts) can determine the need for analysis. The regulatory review programs in the Ford, Carter, and Reagan Administrations have been consistent in this respect--all require analysis of major regulations, generally those with an economic effect of $100 million or more. Second, if a program is projected to have a long life, it is necessary to quantify the future impacts in terms of present values. Third, if the issue is politically charged, CBA can lend a degree of objectivity and structure to the debate.[87]

A well-structured CBA must contain a statement of the problem, alternative solutions, costs and benefits of each alternative, and an explanation of the choice of one alternative over the others.[88] Discussions of each of these points follows, but they are only intended to be a primer or introduction to CBA. There are many cost-benefit textbooks that can be consulted for greater detail.

Problem Statement

A prerequisite for policy analysis is that the issue at hand must be understood. The problem statement structures the analysis. The problem, as well as its significance, causes and effects, and as potential solutions must be presented. This statement also should contain a discussion of legal, economic, and institutional constraints on any possible solution. Furthermore, there should be an explanation of the necessity and basis of government intervention.[89] The statement is a brief, compelling argument justifying the path an analysis will follow. Without an adequate discussion of the issues, the CBA can veer in the wrong direction and be useless or misleading.

Alternatives

The CBA must propose and compare a number of alternative regulatory plans.[90] The alternative of inaction (maintaining the status quo) must be included as a reference point to enable the evaluation of any proposed action. The reader will recall that OMB suggested the following four categories of alternatives:

1. no regulation;
2. major alternatives outside the scope of legislative authority;
3. alternatives within legislative authority; and,
4. market-oriented regulation, such as labeling, performance standards, and incentives.[91]

Every alternative should receive the same attention in the analysis.

Valuation and Monetization of Impacts

Perhaps the most important (and controversial) step in CBA is the identification and measurement of impacts. Secondary effects, linkages, or feedbacks, as well as primary impacts, must be identified. These impacts can be quantified in either nominal or real terms. Nominal monetary impacts occurring over time are unadjusted for the effects of inflation; real monetary impacts are expressed in constant dollars--which includes the effect of a decrease in the purchasing power of a dollar over time. No matter which method is adopted, it must be consistent; all benefits, costs, and discount rates (see below) used in the analysis must be expressed consistently in either real or constant terms. Yet, the OMB Guidance calls for constant dollar values of impacts and a 10 percent discount rate which might be a nominal rate.

Distinguishing Costs, Benefits, and Transfers. The impacts of each alternative must be classified correctly. Creation of goods and services is a benefit. The loss or consumption of societal resources is a cost. Resources that simply move among groups are considered to be income transfer payments and should not be treated as either a benefit or cost. These types of payments have distributional impacts on society and should only be evaluated in that light.

Valuation in Perfect Markets. Consumption, production, and distribution of economic goods and services are broad characteristics of economic behavior. Underlying these characteristics are myriad decisions made by households, businesses, and government aimed at maximizing individual welfare. When few market imperfections exist, market prices can be used to guage the social value (welfare) of impacts because the free interplay of market demand and supply establishes prices in an impersonal and nonpolitical way,[92] reflecting consumers' willingness to pay for goods and services and the opportunity costs of resources.[93]

The fundamental reason for expressing impacts in terms of dollars--when it is appropriate to do so--is to enable a comparison of benefits and costs and to permit the computation of net benefits. Net benefits equal total benefits minus total costs. Efforts should be made to delineate between quoted market prices and maximum prices that consumers are willing to pay. The difference between these two sets of prices reflects consumer surplus. An increase in consumer surplus represents the value of the benefits received from the introduction of a program, project, or regulation. In most cases, maximum prices are difficult to determine; consequently, impacts are likely to be valued using quoted market prices alone, and such estimates should be considered minimum values. On the supply side, quoted market prices (costs) for purchased resources are opportunity costs.

Valuation in Imperfect Markets. Market imperfections can arise from a lack of information about products, monopoly power exercised by businesses and unions, and externalities (the failure to include all social costs--such as pollution--and social benefits in the pricing mechanism). When major market imperfections exist, quoted market prices cannot be used to represent the opportunity costs of resources expended on a program or project. Therefore, shadow prices must be estimated to ascertain opportunity costs. The shadow price of labor would be the hourly wage that workers would be willing to accept in exchange for their labor. Union wage scales often are far above what workers are willing to accept. An hourly wage received in excess of this should be recognized as a transfer payment--from the employer if it is absorbed by a firm and from the consumer if it is passed on in higher prices.

Secondary Markets. A project or regulation may directly affect a few markets or a single market. However, impacts often "ripple" outward to indirectly affect a large number of secondary markets. Because secondary effects are difficult to identify and predict, they present problems for the analyst. These impacts might be counted twice if the analyst fails to discern between manifestations of an initial impact and secondary effects.[94] This can, perhaps, be avoided if the search for potential secondary effects is limited to those markets (often for substitute or complementary goods) where there is a change in price attributable to primary impacts.

Nonmarket Impacts. The absence of existing market values--prices and costs--or a lack of data often can impede or prevent monetization of certain impacts. Socio-political or ethical considerations also may constrain quantification, for example in valuing human lives. The number of lives saved may be estimable, but comparing this to resources expended requires that a dollar value be placed on the lives. Those impacts that cannot be valued in an economic sense must not be ignored or considered valueless. Most cost-benefit manuals require that these at least be mentioned and discussed and included in a summary of costs and benefits. Chapter 4 outlines several alternatives to CBA, where quantification of these types of impacts is not as crucial.

Discounting Cost and Benefit Streams

In any investment or regulatory action, the policymaker must choose among alternatives that have future costs and benefits. Discounting gives present value to future impacts, thereby allowing comparisons of alternatives in the present. There are two general types of discount rates--the opportunity cost of capital and the social discount rate. Each has merit, but they are based on different assumptions and value judgements.

Opportunity Cost of Capital. In general, the opportunity cost method of discounting impacts of public programs reflects the efficiency criterion that the marginal yield on public and private investments be equal. It is based on three principles: 1) public and private investment opportunities are the same; 2) the discount rate represents allocative efficiency in all markets; and, 3) there are no market imperfections that require public investment. There are obvious problems with these assertions. The opportunities, and certainly the obligations, of public and private investment are not always the same. Also, private industry, with little incentive to put a high value on future returns and costs, discounts these very quickly in its investment decision. Thus, the discount rate in the private sector is relatively high.

The opportunity cost of capital probably is inappropriate for most governmental investment decisions. Since it drastically reduces the present value of future impacts, the incentive to engage in long-term investments is distorted. Furthermore, it avoids the valid contention that governmental responsibilities extend far beyond those of private industry. Perhaps governments, in certain functions, should be run more like businesses, but they should not always use the same investment criteria.

It generally is accepted, on the other hand, that the government should ensure that future benefits and costs receive sufficient consideration. This implies that the public sector, in practice, should use a lower discount rate (which will discount future impacts less heavily) than the private sector. Therefore, relying upon a social discount rate may be better suited to evaluating federal government regulations.

<u>Social Discount Rate</u>. The social discount rate is the rate of return required to encourage the level of saving and investment that yields the highest standard of living across future generations. In the United States, this rate has been estimated to be 3 1/2 percent.[95] It is considerably lower than the opportunity cost of capital so it gives greater value to future benefits and costs.

Distribution

Few government programs equally affect all groups in society. Generally, benefits accrue to specific groups, or groups gain at the expense of others. Thus, the issue is either who is the recipient of the benefit and who bears the cost, or who comes out ahead or behind in a transfer of resources. If the contemplated program is intended to be redistributive, analysts may choose to weight the impacts accordingly, giving greater value to gains by the targeted groups. Because distributional issues are not readily apparent in the final CBA calculation, it is imperative that regulatory analysis goes beyond this and gives weight to distributional aspects of government actions.

Uncertainty

Where uncertainty exists, usually due to a lack of data or experience regarding the occurrence of a cost, benefit, or the magnitude of a cost or benefit, there is a set of possible events, each of which could occur but are mutually exclusive. CBA deals with this situation through sensitivity analysis. For each scenario, the projected outcome should be presented. If one alternative prevails (i.e., net benefits always are maximized) through all the scenarios, that alternative is said to be "insensitive" to the uncertainty. Where the solution is sensitive, however, the analyst should go further and assign likely probabilities to each event. The analysis then can be weighted according to the likelihood of the event's occurrence.[96] When conducting a sensitivity analysis, the analyst must identify the source of the uncertainty.

To reiterate, CBA is useful only insofar as it aids and informs decisionmaking. To do so, each study must present all information clearly and logically. Every alternative and its impacts should be systematically presented. The analysis then can be understood and judged on its own merits by independent reviewers. A rationale for choosing one alternative over the others also is imperative. Usually, this is the alternative with the greatest net present value. Theory and reality, however, often do not coincide; not all alternatives can be considered, and not all impacts can be predicted, identified, or quantified. Regulatory impact analysis in these cases (and there are few situations where analysts have complete and perfect information) cannot be objective and thus should not be used as a decision rule.

CONFORMANCE OF THE RIAs WITH OMB GUIDANCE

It is obvious from the Regulatory Impact Analyses (RIAs) that agencies do not follow the same procedures or expend equal effort in preparing the RIAs. The RIAs range in quality from those which are terribly simplistic and perfunctory to those which are so complex that they serve to hide more information than they present. There are great differences in quality among the RIAs produced by different agencies, and differences can be found within an agency or even a single RIA. Many suffer with respect to style and continuity; others do not even resemble cost-benefit studies in form.

As discussed earlier, the OMB guidelines require an RIA to allow "independent reviewers to make an informed judgement that the objectives of E.O. 12291 are satisfied."[97] In addition, an RIA should include

1. a statement of need for and consequences of the proposal;
2. an examination of alternative approaches;
3. an analysis of benefits and costs of the proposal and the alternatives, including net benefit estimates;
4. a rationale for choosing the proposed regulatory action; and,
5. a statement explaining the agency's statutory authority for the proposed regulation.[98]

Allow for Independent Review

Even though many RIAs do not conform with the Executive Order, they at least allow independent reviewers to make this judgement. Independent review would be much easier, however, if the RIAs were organized in terms of the outline specified by OMB. The Farmers Home Administration (FmHA) of the Department of Agriculture (USDA) does this admirably, and the result is a series of well-organized reports. (These fail in other respects, though. They usually lack detail and are much too short and simplistic.)

An orderly format would be especially helpful for complex and technical RIAs. These often provide so much detail and documentation that the quantity of tables, graphs, and detailed discussion of relatively obscure points is distracting. The Department of Transportation (DOT) RIA concerning automatic automobile passenger restraints[99] and the Department of Interior (DOI) RIA on the prohibition of hydrocarbon exploration in two California ocean sanctuaries[100] are too long and detailed. In the latter, the two locations are dealt with separately, even though similar (and often identical) discussions are offered for both. It seems that the analysis could have been condensed. In general, many tables and graphs could have been placed in appendices, rather than in the narrative. In this way, the information would be available without being overwhelming.

Statement of Need For and Consequences of the Proposal

The OMB requires this statement to identify the problem that needs to be corrected and to explain how the regulatory proposal would solve or alleviate the situation. All the RIAs in the study explain why the regulation is being promulgated. Even the most perfunctory RIAs fulfill this requirement. Some of the rules that are deregulatory in nature explain that the problem to be corrected is one of excessive regulatory burden and compliance costs.

Examination of Alternative Approaches

The OMB calls for the presentation and consideration of an excellent range of alternatives, but, unfortunately, no RIA mentioned in this study follows this suggestion. Most either offer alternative levels of stringency or measure costs and benefits under various effective dates.

Although the guidelines call for agencies to consider alternatives outside the authority granted in the enabling statute, many writers indicated that they felt bound by the wording of the act. The FmHA, for example, in an RIA on a revision of the definition of "low income" for a rural housing program, failed to consider this type of alternative, merely stating that "because the legislation is fairly specific in its requirements, the options will have similar effects."[101]

In addition, few RIAs include market-oriented alternatives, such as market-incentive strategies. For example, an RIA by DOI examining changes in the fees and rental structures for the noncompetitive onshore oil and gas leasing program does not include competitive bidding as an alternative.[102]

The Federal Aviation Administration (FAA) of DOT, on the other hand, includes market-based alternatives in an RIA of a regulation to minimize congestion and environmental damage (primarily noise pollution) at Washington's National Airport. One alternative presented is to increase the landing fees while reducing the quota of landing slots for each airline. This could encourage airlines to drop less profitable routes to and from the city, reducing congestion and noise without a comparable loss of service.[103]

Estimation of Benefits and Costs

The OMB guidelines state that the present value of all potential real benefits and costs realized in the future should be measured in constant dollars and should be discounted at a rate of 10 percent. Other discount rates can be used to test sensitivities, if desired.[104] Net benefits also should be computed for each alternative.

Even though the guidelines explicitly warn agencies not to include transfer payments as real costs and/or benefits, some RIAs fail in this regard. Some treat increased government revenue and lower wages (paid by businesses, including government contractors) as benefits, without accounting for the reduced after-tax income of workers. All of these impacts are transfer payments.

Many RIAs fail to extend benefits and costs into the future. Those that do often fail to measure the impacts in constant dollars as OMB specifies. OMB requires RIAs to use constant dollar measures for future benefits and costs, discounted at 10 percent. It is quite possible, from the discussion of discount rates above, that this is inappropriately high. All agencies that discount future impacts use the 10 percent rate. Some use more than one discount rate to test overall sensitivity. The shortcomings of the RIAs regarding estimates of costs and benefits will be studied in more detail later in this chapter.

Rationale for the Final Decision

The guidelines imply that the best regulatory alternative should be chosen on the basis of largest net benefits, except where this would be prohibited by law.[105] According to OMB, CBA should be the decisionmaking rationale, rather than a tool to facilitate decisionmaking. Most CBA manuals, however, agree that public policy decisions should not be based strictly on cost-benefit studies.

Not all of the RIAs base the preferred alternative on CBA. The RIA detailing the decision to rescind the automatic passenger restraint requirement is a well-known example. Although rescission is not considered in the analysis as an alternative, the National Highway Traffic Safety Administration (NHTSA) concluded in the RIA that

> The Agency's quantitative analysis of the hypothetical costs and benefits of the standard leads it to the conclusion that viewed only on those grounds, the standard need not necessarily be rejected. But the Agency must also consider whether consumers will accept or reject automatic restraints.[106]

In the FmHA RIA redefining low income, the agency determined that one of the options would result in the least cost to the government, while benefiting the greatest percentage of the population. This alternative was rejected, however, because another "complies with the intent of the law...and limits the program to those applicants that would most likely be unable to qualify for housing without government assistance."[107] In this case, the agency justified its decision on the basis of distributional issues (and most would agree that it was correct in doing so), rather than on the basis of the greatest net benefits to society. This raises the question, again, of whether the maximization of net benefits is the best criterion for evaluating some redistributive regulatory programs. Considering that OMB requires such a wide variety of alternatives, sole reliance on the criterion of allocative efficiency may be singularly inappropriate.

Statutory Authority Cited

The guidelines require an agency to certify that the chosen alternative is within the agency's statutory authority. Since few of the RIAs consider alternatives lying outside the scope of legal authority, in practice this seems to be a superfluous requirement. Were agencies to include the wide range of alternatives specified, it, of course, would be necessary. Many cited in the statement of need the legislative act calling for the regulation. Without exception, the RIAs cited the statutory authority.

RIA CONFORMANCE WITH COST-BENEFIT STANDARDS

There remains a more critical test that the RIAs must pass: do the agencies perform CBA in conformance with generally accepted cost-benefit standards? As stated before, these standards should be applied to deregulatory actions, as well as to rules increasing the level of regulation.

It has been shown that the OMB guidelines in some instances do not ensure good CBA. Predictably, the RIAs written in accordance with E.O. 12291 do not conform with accepted cost-benefit standards. In general, the RIAs display a bias toward deregulation and often are written as justifications of regulatory decisions. This section will evaluate the RIAs in eight areas:

1. discussion of the problem and regulatory issue;

2. examination of alternatives;

3. estimation of costs;

4. estimation of benefits;

5. treatment of transfer payments;

6. inclusion of equity and distributional issues;

7. treatment of uncertainty; and,

8. discounting procedure.

Discussion of the Problem and Regulatory Issue

A good RIA provides all of the general information a reader needs to become acquainted with the issue. The discussion of the issue should include a description of other regulations in the same policy area, including those issued by other agencies and departments. Historical background information about an agency's own regulatory involvement also should be provided. Finally, as required by OMB, this section should include a description of the need for the new level of regulation and the predicted results. Again, this section should not be lengthy or detract from the CBA; it should be brief but information packed.

FAA's RIA on congestion and environmental damage at the Washington National Airport, for the most part, discusses the regulatory issue well. Especially impressive is the study's concise description of how the proposed regulation may affect airport operations, airline service, and passenger behavior. However, although the goals of the regulation include the reduction of noise pollution, the RIA fails to state why this is necessary and desirable.[108]

The perfunctory RIAs, some less than ten pages long, do not and cannot adequately present the regulatory issue. Some merely state how the new regulation would differ from the old standard and why the change is an improvement.

Examination of Alternatives

Good CBA requires an in-depth examination of a wide range of alternatives. Unfortunately, agencies often present alternatives that can easily be disposed of, thus "proving" that the proposed regulation is the best alternative. In these instances, the alternatives are not presented and considered in good faith.

In DOI's RIA examining changes in the administration of noncompetitive oil and gas leases, one alternative is to require each applicant to submit the payment of the first year's rent. The agency would return this advanced payment to all unsuccessful applicants after thirteen weeks (in the meantime investing the money, earning float revenue). Although this would be an inappropriate policy for the government to follow, and eventually the RIA acknowledges this, the scheme is still included as an alternative.[109]

Another problem in the area of alternatives is that in some cases the alternatives are not discussed in sufficient detail. In one instance, alternatives are not even mentioned, although the RIA implies that options were considered. In this FmHA RIA for a regulation modifying the criteria for processing Rural Housing Loan Assistance applications, in each of seven areas the agency simply describes the chosen option, without mentioning any of the options that were rejected.[110]

In another FmHA RIA, only two alternatives are considered. The agency had the option to grant an interest-credit subsidy to moderate income rural housing borrowers. In this two-page RIA, the alternatives are either to grant the subsidy or not to grant it. The agency did not perform the analysis in good faith, as the range of alternatives indicates.[111] In its defense, however, this may have been a case where the enabling legislation was so specific that CBA was not appropriate.

In some cases, the alternatives are limited to indefinite levels of stringency. For example, in a National Oceanic and Atmospheric Administration (NOAA) RIA for a regulation to license and facilitate deep seabed mining exploration, the three alternatives are fixed regulations, flexible regulations preceding license issuance, and flexible regulations both preceding and following license issuance. NOAA determined, without quantification, that different stringency levels are necessary for different provisions of the regulation.[112]

A better treatment of alternatives is found in a DOI RIA. The Department has great flexibility in regulating the procedures, conditions, and stringency of regulations for competitive bidding on some Alaskan oil and gas leases. In each of these three areas of flexibility, the agency treats the alternatives differently. DOI determined that variable bonus bidding, with low fixed royalties, is the best procedure. Elements of the condition of the sale--tract size, period of the lease, allowance of joint bidding, criteria for accepting a bid, and protection of cultural and environmental values--were set to result in a maximum net benefit to society. Again, many alternatives are considered. The RIA also considers three alternatives relating to the stringency of the new regulation. While the RIA lacks quantification, it is strong in its range of alternatives.[113]

Estimation of Costs

For those rules increasing the level of regulation, cost estimates often include costs incurred by business and government. Compliance costs (such as for record keeping and reporting), increased production costs (carefully excluding transfer payments, such as increased wages or taxes), and other efficiency losses should be noted. The costs of a rule reducing the level of regulation must include the value of the loss of protection to groups formerly benefiting from regulation. (Quite often this is one side of a transfer payment.) This last measure often is absent in the RIAs.

The bias toward deregulation is discernible in the discussion of costs. The DOT RIA for the regulation rescinding the requirement for automatic passenger restraints is an example. The RIA displays extensive analysis of the industry's compliance costs, which, when the rule is suspended, represent benefits to society. The RIA does not, however, consider the quantified costs of rescinding the regulation. In an appendix, the analysis states that "the conversion of safety benefits (i.e., lives saved and injuries avoided) into dollar values is an improper and inappropriate method of reaching decisions on safety issues" because it is "offensive" and such a large range of values historically have been used.[114] The agency eventually does quantify the benefits of "a hypothetical reduction of fatalities and injuries" for three alternatives to rescission (including the existing rule), all of which uphold the requirement for restraints and only differ in the timing of the implementation.[115] If we can assume that societal benefits of the current rule (reduced fatalities and injuries) will become societal costs of the rescission of the rule, it should be possible to compare the costs and benefits of rescission. The RIA does not take this logical step, however.

The bias also is evident in a Department of Labor (DOL) RIA of a regulation reducing affirmative action reporting requirements that would exempt many smaller businesses with government contracts from submitting affirmative action plans (AAPs). According to the RIA, the new requirement will "relieve nearly 75 percent of federal contractors from AAP requirements...[but] about 76.7 percent of employees will remain covered" (i.e., their employers must submit AAPs).[116] The RIA gives rough estimates of cost savings to both the contractors and the government from the changes in reporting requirements. However, there is no discussion of the costs to society of the changes. These could be significant and certainly should not be ignored. For example, there is no discussion of the possibility that those employees no longer covered may need the protection of the reporting requirement the most.

DOL is not the only department that fails to properly define costs. The USDA frequently defines costs in terms of the reduction in costs (which technically are benefits).[117] If nothing else, this inconsistent use of basic terminology can be misleading or confusing.

The only RIA in this study that considers the important concept of consumer surplus is the DOT study of Washington National Airport. The cost to passengers who lose access to air service because of the regulation is estimated by calculating the loss in consumer surplus. In addition, the RIA correctly includes as a cost the inconvenience (access cost) incurred by passengers forced to use nearby airports. The RIA monetizes these and other costs for each of the alternatives. It also determines total costs, benefits, and net benefits for each of the alternatives.[118] It is one of the very few RIAs to display information in such a clear and concise manner.

DOL tends to completely ignore the costs implicit in deregulatory actions. In two RIAs--one for a regulation reducing the definition of "prevailing wage" in the Davis-Bacon statutory requirement for wage levels in government projects and the AAP reporting requirement noted above--the Department fails to quantify or even identify costs. It only uses the word "cost" when referring to cost savings (benefits).[119]

The OMB guidelines do not encourage agencies to include secondary costs. None of the RIAs seriously consider secondary costs, such as reductions in efficiency and incentives. The same can be said, in general, for nonmonetary costs. Usually, when an agency notes a nonmonetary cost, it is describing, instead, a distributional impact or transfer payment.

Estimation of Benefits

Benefits, in the case of a rule that would increase the level of regulation, are typically a measurement of the resources that are preserved or protected. Most regulations of this type deal with environmental issues.

Many of these benefits are, by nature, hard to quantify, although some RIAs show more courage in this than others do. RIAs for rules that reduce the level of regulation should include as benefits, among other things, the reduction in compliance costs.

The RIAs for the latter type of regulation are quite extensive in their calculation of the cost savings of reduced paperwork, secretarial and managerial time saved, and reduced government costs for monitoring compliance. An example of a more complete benefit estimation for a deregulatory act is in a DOT RIA for a regulation that would reduce the 5 miles per hour (m.p.h.) car bumper standard to 2.5 m.p.h. Benefits include lower gasoline consumption due to the reduced bumper weight; consumer price savings (the new bumpers would be less expensive to manufacture and the auto makers claim that the savings would be passed on to consumers); finance charges saved due to lower car prices (although part of this is a transfer from the lending institutions); and long-term tooling cost savings. The RIA also cites nonquantifiable benefits, such as oil conservation in the national interest and conformance with international bumper standards.[120]

As in the case of cost estimation, many RIAs indicate that the analysts had trouble distinguishing benefits from transfer payments. The FmHA RIA for the redefinition of low income for its loan program tries to avoid this distinction by identifying only "impacts." According to the RIA, "the economic impacts of setting low income levels will be on borrower housing and spendable income, value of real estate, rural areas, geographic distribution of funds, and racial distribution of funds."[121] While the agency does not quantify these "impacts," it correctly does not define them as benefits or costs to society. However, the RIA does not discuss the potential benefits and costs, such as a change in administrative costs.

The tendency to ignore certain measurements that are uncertain is evident in a DOI RIA discussing limits on oil and gas activity in two coastal zones in California. The RIA states that the costs (foregone energy resources) of this action cannot be compared to the benefits (preservation of the biomass from potential production accidents) because

1. there is a large range of estimates for the value of the organisms because there are so many methods of determining their value.

2. there is a wide range of value estimates for the hydrocarbon resources because future prices are uncertain and no exploratory drilling has been permitted that would help determine the quantity of hydrocarbon resources present.

3. the two resources have different life-cycles. Development of the hydrocarbons would occur over about twenty years while the life-cycle of the biomass is infinite.

4. the biomass will only represent a societal cost if an accident occurs in the development of hydrocarbon sources.[122]

Because of these factors, the RIA serves only to inform decisionmakers of the various factors involved and not their magnitude.

CBA can deal with these uncertainties, although it cannot provide specific values, of course. Sensitivity analysis can provide a range of values for the biomass and for the quantity of hydrocarbon resources present (using data from nearby areas where testing and development is underway). The RIA merely presents these possible values and fails to proceed beyond this point. Future prices for hydrocarbon products can be estimated from various industry and independent studies and price models. The problem of noncorresponding lifecycles can be overcome by determining present values of each, using an appropriate discount rate. The agency could have dealt with the fourth area of uncertainty with the use of a probability or risk factor. In short, any benefit or cost estimate is better than none.

In contrast to secondary cost estimates, secondary benefits are more likely to be included in an RIA. For example, an RIA by the NOAA for a regulation that would permit and encourage commercial development of ocean thermal energy conversion (OTEC) includes as benefits new competition with imported oil and new export possibilities. One secondary benefit, correctly identified, is "major expansion opportunities for other sectors of the U.S. economy."[123] However, it must be pointed out that the RIA incorrectly lists several transfer payments (tax revenues and alternative means of production of energy intensive products) as indirect benefits.[124] None of the RIAs in the study attempt to use willingness-to-pay pricing for benefits.

Correct Treatment of Transfer Payments

Many instances of incorrect classification of transfer payments as costs or benefits have been noted. One of the few RIAs that correctly identifies a transfer payment is a DOL study specifying the level of employment at which a pension fund can suspend benefits to working retirees. On a rather minor point, the RIA identifies pension payouts as transfer payments. Throughout the RIA, however, the agency considers the part-time work of the retirees as a net benefit to society.[125] This only can be true if there is no unemployment. If unemployment <u>does</u> exist, a new worker can add to the national economy only if he or she <u>is</u> filling a newly created job and does not displace another worker. If not, the wages paid to the retiree represent a transfer payment from one worker to another. Therefore, this RIA identifies one transfer payment yet misses another.

Discussion of Equity and Distributional Issues

Most of the RIAs make statements about equity and distributional issues, usually in connection with an incorrect identification of resource transfers. One RIA previously noted, FmHA's RIA on the new definition of low income, bases its final decision on a distributional argument. On the other hand, DOL fails to discuss the distributional implications for wage earners in two RIAs and for minorities in another.[126]

Correct Treatment of Uncertainty

Sensitivity analysis is the accepted method for treating uncertain assumptions and estimates. For example, the NOAA ocean sanctuary RIA should have overcome any hesitancy to quantify costs and benefits by using a range of values to estimate the value of hydrocarbon and biomass resources.[127]

RIAs at the other extreme choose one questionable value for an uncertain variable, without testing the results using other estimates. The DOL RIA concerning the suspension of pension benefits typifies this. The RIA seeks to define employment for the purpose of suspension of pension benefits. Forty hours per month is determined to be the "employment cliff," beyond which pensioners' benefits are suspended. Retirees who had worked in a company that offered a multiemployer pension fund lose their benefits if they are reemployed in the same industry. If these workers choose to work after retirement, therefore, they must obtain jobs in another industry. On the basis of a single study, DOL chose $10 per hour as the most likely new wage:

> The only union scale figure in the Handbook of Labor Statistics was for journeymen which was $11 per hour in 1978. Taking this number to be representatives (sic) of the union scale paid by multiemployer plan sponsors and adjusted for inflation this wage translates to approximately $15 per hour in 1981.[128]

DOL had previously determined that these pensioners would have to accept a one-third wage reduction in the new job; hence, the new wage would most likely be $10 per hour. DOL also had estimated that a pensioner would not seek to earn more than the Social Security earnings limit, $5,000 per year. As a result, DOL set the employment cliff at forty hours per month--roughly $5,000 divided by twelve months divided by $10 per hour.[129] This RIA sets the level on the basis of a few rough estimates, whereas a sensitivity analysis would have been appropriate for the two-thirds estimate and the $15 wage. In summary, analysts too often randomly perform sensitivity tests, without stating why it is necessary or why certain estimates are possibly imprecise. Some performed so many sensitivity tests that they seemed to be certain of nothing. In contrast, some analysts failed to use the technique when they should have.

Proper Discounting Procedure

OMB's prescription of the 10 percent discount rate probably biases many analyses in favor of deregulation. The RIAs that use discounting usually rely on this figure. However, most use more than one rate, ranging from 5 to 15 percent. These claim to be testing the sensitivity of the results to a changing discount rate but do not explain why the 10 percent level may be incorrect or even what the discount rate signifies. It would seem that the choice of a discount rate should not be terribly uncertain.

One exception is the DOT bumper standards RIA. This analysis discusses the issue of using the social rate of time preference as a discount rate. Ultimately, though, it decides to stay with the 10 percent level because "the bumper standard is a consumer expenditure in the private marketplace."[130] Therefore, a discount rate more closely reflecting opportunity costs, in this case, is appropriate. The argument has merit and, more important, the discussion shows that the authors knew the reasons for discounting.

Summary of RIA Quality

It seems that many of the RIAs merely serve as justifications for the activities an agency wishes to carry out. A deregulatory bias is apparent in many of the studies. While some RIAs may provide excellent analyses of some points, none of them totally comply with either OMB guidelines or with generally-accepted cost-benefit standards. Many of the authors do not seem to be familiar with these techniques--especially the crucial distinctions between transfer payments and benefits or costs. Determining a proper discount rate for estimating present values also seems to be a problem area.

Another conclusion that can be drawn from this study is that CBA is not the correct way to evaluate some regulations. Three instances come immediately to mind. First, social welfare programs are not designed to maximize benefits to society as a whole. Their purpose is to improve the welfare of a certain group within society. It seems rather callous to base a program of this type only on its effects on society as a whole. Second, in the case of many environmental or health-related regulations, often the impact that is to be avoided through regulation is a catastrophic event that should be prevented at all costs. In these cases, CBA appears to an inappropriate way of judging public regulation. Finally, too often the legislative mandate specifies the precise level of benefits (i.e., the goal). In this case, CBA is unnecessary and a more appropriate evaluation tool would be cost-effectiveness analysis.

CONCLUSION

Quantitative analysis of public policy has existed in theory and application for several decades (see Appendix 3). Only recently, however, has CBA been required of all executive departments. CBA, properly perceived and performed, can greatly assist decisionmaking. Unfortunately, the response to the initiative of Executive Order 12291 has been poor.

OMB, in its elaboration of E.O. 12291, has not provided an adequate framework for the agencies. The agencies, in general, have not provided the necessary guidance to their analysts. An examination of the RIAs performed in fulfillment of the Order reveals the result. Although the RIAs vary greatly in quality, none completely meets the requirements of an ideal CBA. Part of this problem can be attributed to the lack of proper guidance. There also may be a lack of incentive to spend resources on these studies. As the GAO pointed out, agencies, due to OMB waiver procedures, may not take the requirement seriously.

The poor quality of the RIAs may be due to the failure of CBA theory to encompass all regulatory issues. This is a failure of E.O. 12291 as well. By apparently requiring that regulatory decisions be made on rational economic efficiency grounds, it obscures the fact that regulation is the implementation of congressional and executive values. The stated goals of E.O. 12291 can be valid and worthwhile but only if these shortcomings are realized and, hopefully, corrected.

Finally, the main point of this paper is that CBA is not necessarily an objective policymaking tool when it is used to evaluate public regulation. To the extent that anyone claims that it is or presents it as such, it can be misused.

CHAPTER 4
REFINEMENTS TO THE REGULATORY PROCESS

INTRODUCTION

The purpose of this chapter is twofold. First, it presents a new recommended federal regulatory process. Second, it discusses alternative analytical techniques to be used in conjunction with the process.

As have all recent presidents, Ronald Reagan has made refinements to the system of executive oversight of the federal regulatory process. His system imposes, in many cases, a rigid cost-benefit analysis (CBA) framework to evaluate existing and proposed rules. This strategy implies that the review is objective and scientific.

Politics, however, must enter the regulatory process; this cannot be avoided. The Administration's hesitancy to regulate the private markets stems from both ideological and pragmatic concerns. To be sure, the Administration acknowledges that, in certain instances, limited federal regulation is necessary. However, in general, it believes that less regulation will improve private sector cash flow, reduce inflationary pressure, and encourage private initiative. While many may disagree with this stance, or feel that regulatory goals override these considerations, the fact that the President has the authority to oversee much of the regulatory system suggests that a more appropriate framework is needed to address public concerns about pending and existing regulations. The framework must not challenge the authority of the executive regulatory agencies, however.

The recommended federal regulatory process, discussed in the following pages, offers a proper balance between the varied public and government interests. The system would result in rulemaking that is less time consuming, more coherent, and more effective than presently is the case.

THE PROCESS REDEFINED

Objectives

Unify the Process. The regulatory process has evolved from administration to administration. In the past, each agency created an identity and structure tailored to meet its specific needs. Little attention has been given to how agency objectives or operations fit into the government structure as a whole. This has resulted in a collage of government regulations that are possibly repetitious, unnecessary, and ineffective. Through unifying the structural process by which all executive agencies promulgate regulation, the problems of overlap and waste might be eliminated, while maintaining the correct balance between agency authority and administrative policy.

Simplify the Process. In order to unify the process by which agencies establish and maintain effective regulatory procedures, a simple but effective foundation must be laid for all agencies to follow. Simplifying the regulatory process will save time and money and increase predictability. A sound agency regulatory pattern must be established and maintained.

Greater Public Awareness. The third objective of the proposed regulatory process is to generate greater public awareness. This will be accomplished by documenting and publicizing the entire agency proposal and review process. Presently, only the initial and final regulatory proposals and rules are published. Increased public access to the dialogue between the agency and the administration would cause greater responsiveness, greater agency objectiveness, and more effective regulation. At the same time, greater public interest in the regulatory process would be generated.

The following proposal accomplishes these goals and, yet, makes a minimum number of changes in the existing process. It is composed of two phases: phase one, referred to as "Announcement and Classification," and phase two, called "Analysis and Comment." Both phases will be illustrated by symbolic flow charts, Figures 6 and 7. Narrative discussion of the phase will follow each illustration.

Figure 6
The Proposed System, Phase One:
Announcement and Classification

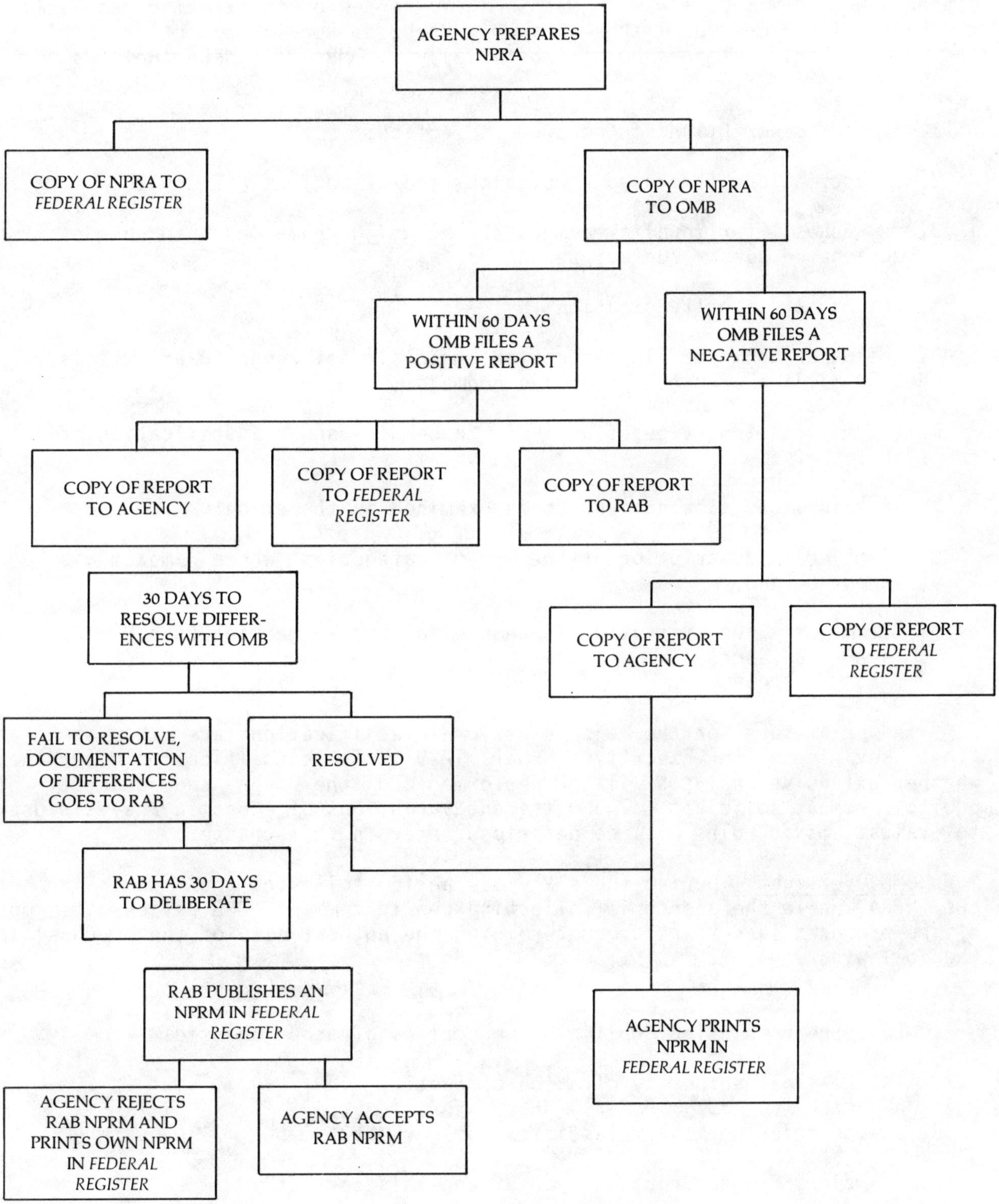

Phase One: Announcement and Classification

Proposed Rule Announced. Once an agency decides to take regulatory action, whether it be a new regulation or a review of an existing regulation, the agency first must publish a Notice of Proposed Regulatory Action (NPRA) in the Federal Register and submit it officially to OMB. The NPRA includes

1. a brief description of the proposed action;
2. a description of related regulations and/or actions (if any);
3. a request for public comment, including name and address of designated agency contact person;
4. the legal authority citation;
5. the major/nonmajor classification: major if net economic affect is \$100 million or more, otherwise nonmajor;
6. if major, the type of analysis to be done and a justification of this choice;
7. if major, the alternatives to be examined in the study;
8. if major, a description of the broad categories where impact is expected; and,
9. if major, the tentative schedule for public hearing (set 90-120 days in advance).

The parameters for the major/nonmajor classification are the same as those set forth in Executive Order 12291. The classification determines whether extensive analysis will be performed and the type and quantity of public comment solicited. The different variations of economic analysis used to evaluate major rules will be described later in this chapter.

OMB Oversight. During the sixty-day period following the submission of the NPRA, while the agency is collecting public comment, OMB reviews its copy of the proposed agency action, determining the authenticity of the proposal in the following ways:

1. Does the regulation duplicate the actions of other agencies?
2. Is the legal authority citation correct?
3. Is the major/nonmajor classification correct?
4. If major, is the proposed type of analysis correct?

By the end of sixty days, OMB submits a report of its findings to the agency. If OMB feels that the agency is incorrect in these areas, it files a positive report with the agency, the Federal Register, and the Regulatory Advisory Board (described below). If OMB has no problems with the NPRA in these four areas, it files a negative report with the agency and in the Federal Register.

Following the receipt of a positive OMB report, sixty days are allotted to resolve the differences between the NPRA and OMB's report. The agency may exercise its authority to disregard OMB's findings. Nevertheless, OMB's report is duly recorded.

Recording Differences. In the case of a positive OMB report, there is a sixty-day period reserved to settle the differences between the agency and OMB. The first thirty days are designated for communication between the agency and OMB to negotiate a resolution. Official communication between the two is in writing and copies of this correspondence are filed with the Regulatory Advisory Board (RAB). If, after thirty days, a consensus is reached between OMB and the agency, the agency is responsible for printing its Notice of Proposed Rulemaking (NPRM) in the Federal Register. This notice includes

1. a description of planned action;
2. the final classification of major or nonmajor;
3. if major, the date and time of public rulemaking proceedings;
4. if major, details of the analysis to be performed; and,
5. the final legal authority citation.

However, if the agency and OMB fail to agree on the points in the NPRA after thirty days, the dispute is resolved by the Regulatory Advisory Board (RAB). The RAB is envisioned as an independent federal level review board. Its purpose is to render an informed and impartial decision on regulatory differences that arise at certain points in the regulatory review process. The RAB should be composed of an odd number of board members (no more than seven), selected by the Speaker of the House of Representatives, Senate Majority Leader, and President for four-year staggered terms. The Board should consist of representatives of business, labor, and consumers. All should have some background in economics and be familiar with the regulatory process. The RAB would be governed by majority rule, with the chairperson dictating agendas and rules of order.

The RAB would resolve the disputes in phase one only on the basis of written documents; no oral testimony would be offered. A ruling would be forthcoming within thirty days of the receipt of this documentation and would be published in the form of an NPRM in the Federal Register. An agency is not required to recognize the RAB ruling, and may choose, instead, to publish its own NPRM. The system would serve to document disagreement among the agency, OMB, and RAB over the classification of the proposed regulatory action.

Concluding Remarks Regarding Phase One. The first phase of the recommended process differs minimally from the APA. The NPRA and NPRM are similar to the APA's Advanced Notice of Proposed Rulemaking and Notice of Proposed Rulemaking used with informal rulemaking procedures. The critical point in phase one is the classification of a regulation as major or nonmajor. This determines if an analysis must be performed and if a public hearing will be held (in phase two). The unique feature of the recommended process is that any classification differences between OMB and an agency are fully documented, and, if necessary, a final opinion is offered by the RAB.

This procedure, though, implies three changes in the process. First, OMB officially becomes an overseer of the regulatory process. Second, the hybrid rulemaking features of the process, in the case of a major rule, guarantee that a case record will be produced that can be used if the courts decide to review a rule. Third, the public will be more aware of conflicts within the executive branch as regulations are being formed. This increases accountability. Public pressure can keep rulemakers from becoming rulers.

Phase Two: Analysis and Comment

Agency Publishes Regulatory Analysis. Initially in phase two, an agency publishes a summary of the results of a preliminary economic analysis of the regulatory alternatives. This is required only for major regulations. The agency has up to ninety days from the first publication of the NPRA to perform the analysis. Depending on the amount of discretion the agency has, this will be either cost-benefit, cost-effectiveness, or multiobjective analysis. A discussion of each of these is found in the second half of this chapter.

This summary of analytical results is published in the Federal Register and is sent to the appropriate congressional oversight committee(s) and OMB. During the sixty days following publication, comment is received from each of these three sources. Minor rules during phase two will not have an analysis published or a public hearing, but will receive comment from the three sources.

Comments Received on Planned Major Regulation. Following the publication of an agency's preliminary analysis, the appropriate congressional committees have sixty days to submit comments regarding the regulation to the agency and to file copies with the RAB. Presumably these comments will focus on the legislative intent of the enabling legislation. Congressional research agencies may be consulted for information as directed by Congress.

OMB also has sixty days to verify the results of the analysis. Its comments should focus on the analytical technique, for example, problems with the data, assumptions, alternatives, or calculations. OMB also submits a report of its findings to RAB.

Written public comment is received for forty-five days from the time the agency publishes the analytical results. These comments will shed light on the possible impacts on the groups affected. The remaining fifteen days in the sixty-day period are reserved for public hearings, held by the RAB. The RAB determines the length of the hearing.

Figure 7
The Proposed System, Phase Two:
Analysis and Comment

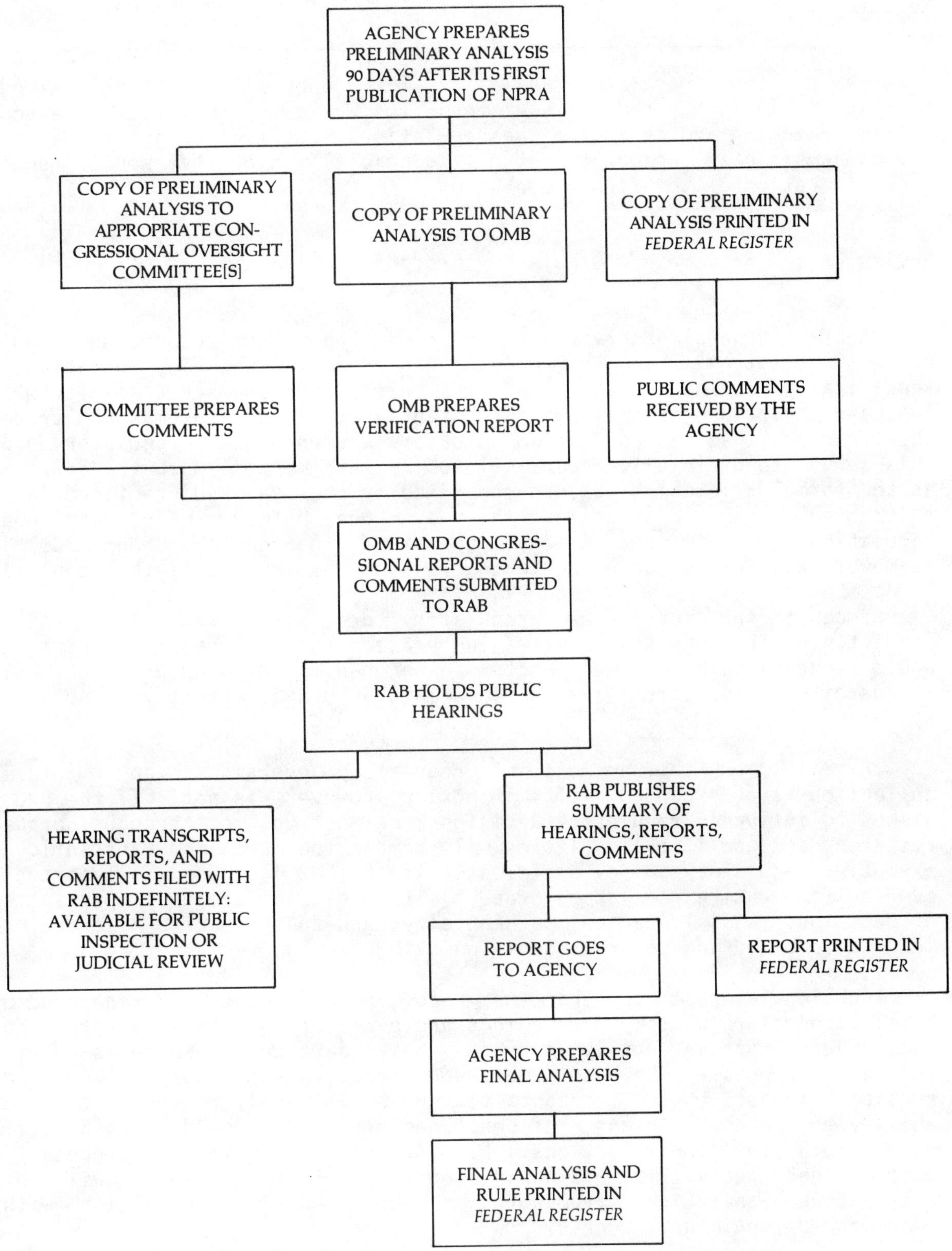

In phase two, therefore, the RAB is responsible for filing and maintaining all documents received and conducting public hearings. The RAB will be required to prepare a summary report based on the hearings and reports. This would be submitted to the agency and printed in the Federal Register.

Final Decision. After receiving the RAB hearing report, the agency must prepare a final regulatory analysis. The agency will print this along with the final rule in the Federal Register. The agency, of course, is responsible for implementing and enforcing the regulation. Short of congressional action, the agency is only subject to potential judicial action that would require a reconsideration of the final regulation.

Review of the Recommended Regulatory Process

A few general observations can be made about the recommended regulatory process. First, it resembles rulemaking procedures now in operation. It specifically is patterned along the rulemaking parameters set forth in the APA, and, therefore, represents a substantive type of rulemaking procedure. The creation of an RAB adds an adjudicatory element to the regulatory process. This serves to officially record all public testimony in much the same manner as the formal rulemaking pattern specified by the APA, and practiced in hybrid rulemaking. The distinction in phase one between major and nonmajor regulations is similar to that contained in Executive Order 12291. This framework also calls for economic analysis of the impacts of the regulation.

Second, the recommended regulatory process is simpler and more predictable than existing rulemaking procedures. All regulatory initiatives would be resolved in a timely matter in an open forum. The process would be standardized and streamlined into a more accurate, effective, and efficient system.

Finally, OMB's functions of regulatory oversight and information collection are expanded. Its authority, however, is not. If the President wishes to influence regulatory decisions, he must do so through persuasion, research and politics. Politics will remain the most important influence on executive regulatory policy decisions. If the OMB is given the opportunity to oversee the entire regulatory process, its review of all the important stages of decisions--classification, authenticity, and analysis of a major rule--will lead to informed and coherent decisionmaking.

Public interest in the the recommended process is enhanced by the publication of regulatory proceedings and by ensuring that interested citizens and groups can personally express their particular concerns during the rulemaking process. The harmony between executive regulatory policy and the public interest that it ought to serve ultimately relies on the public's ability to express opinions, influence decisions, and hold public officials accountable for their actions. Elements of the recommended process promote each of these goals. The following portion of the chapter will discuss alternative analytical frameworks to be used in conjunction with the recommended regulatory process.

ALTERNATIVE ANALYTICAL FRAMEWORKS

Analysis in the Proposed System

The regulatory procedure outlined in the first half of this chapter requires an agency to publish a Notice of Proposed Regulatory Action (NPRA). Among other things, the NPRA should contain an agency classification of major or nonmajor and, if major, the analytical tool that will be used to evaluate it. Chapter 3 explained why CBA may not be an acceptable tool in all cases. Analysis of regulation is essentially a trade-off between the twin evils of excessive quantification and undocumented agency discretion.[131] In other words, in regulatory evaluation, there is a need for objectivity, such as is found in cost-benefit analysis, and a need for description and discretion, for example in weighing redistributive effects. CBA, as prescribed in Executive Order 12291, seems to overquantify. It has been suggested in this study that quantification may be casting a false aura of objectivity over the regulatory decisions. Therefore, the three types of analyses used in the proposed regulatory process have one thing in common--none will be used as a decision rule.

Lester Lave, in The Strategy of Social Regulation: Decision Frameworks for Policy, outlines alternative regulatory "frameworks." These include market regulation, no-risk, risk-benefit, and cost-effectiveness, as well as cost-benefit.[132] These frameworks, along with another, multiobjective analysis, suggest an overall framework for regulatory analysis.

It is proposed that the agencies' regulatory analyses be one of three types--cost-benefit analysis, cost-effectiveness analysis, or multiobjective analysis. In addition, Lave's market regulation and no-risk frameworks suggest the scope of the alternatives that should be considered where possible. Following is a guideline describing which type of analysis is appropriate in which cases. Agencies do not have complete regulatory discretion in many cases. The specificity of the enabling legislation and budgetary restrictions are what will determine the type of analysis to be performed.

Cost-Benefit Analysis. Cost-benefit analysis need not be an abusive analytical technique. When benefits, costs, and risks are general and descriptive, they should not be quantified. Thus, the proposed CBA documentation differs from the executive order version. It becomes more descriptive and, as a result, Lave's risk-benefit framework can fit within this analysis.

The techniques for correct CBA have been described in Chapter 3. It was noted that a cost-benefit study must present costs and benefits logically and clearly, along with uncertainties. Where values are not quantifiable, they should be presented and described. CBA should be used when the goal is not quantitatively precise and where the constraints are not too restrictive.

Cost-Effectiveness Analysis. Cost-effectiveness analysis (CEA) should be the analytical tool when the regulatory goal is explicit and quantitative (e.g., reduce the number of deaths associated with a certain activity or reduce particles per billion of a certain toxic substance) or if the goal is more general within a budgetary constraint (e.g., reduce fatalities to the extent possible, given a certain amount of funds).

According to Quade, CEA "usually consists of an attempt to minimize dollar costs subject to some mission requirement (which may not be measurable in dollar terms) or, conversely, to maximize some physical measure of output subject to a budget constraint."[133] He identifies five steps in CEA:

1. Identify the objectives which you are trying to attain through the policy. Determine how to measure the attainment of the goal.

2. Determine the alternatives, "the means by which it is hoped the objectives can be attained."

3. Identify the costs, "the resources [that] can no longer be used for other purposes." These should be measured as opportunity costs.

4. Use a model to predict costs and the "extent to which each alternative would assist in attaining the objective." The models can range from mathematical equations to computer programs to verbal descriptions.

5. Choose a criterion, "a rule or standard by which to rank the alternatives in order of desirability and choose the most promising."[134]

Lave gives an example of the case where there is a fixed budget and a broad goal--The National Cancer Institute, whose goal is to reduce the number of cancer deaths. The Institute has many programs to achieve cancer reduction--research, public education, reducing exposure to carcinogenic substances, and clinical testing. Each has a different marginal benefit (i.e., number of lives saved by the last dollar spent). CEA requires that the funds be allocated among the programs so that the marginal benefit of resources spent on each program is equal.[135]

The EPA requires cost-effectiveness analysis in instances where "many benefits are not easily quantified, or where a specific objective is mandated by law." EPA's RIA guidelines point out that CEA is valuable in providing two types of comparisons of alternatives. First, it helps identify the most efficient way of reaching a certain level of benefits. Second, it helps identify the policy that maximizes a stated benefit given a resource (compliance cost) constraint.[136] CEA, then, is appropriate where resource constraints are significant or where the goal can be precisely quantified. It does not make a judgement on the regulation itself, only the strategy for reaching the regulatory goal.

<u>Multiobjective Analysis</u>. Multiobjective analysis should be used when more than one objective is to be addressed by the regulatory action. The technique also is useful when there are conflicting benefits and risks (or costs). It can deal with multiple constraints, as well as multiple objectives. Rather than focusing on an optimal solution, the decisionmaker

selects the option which optimizes the net benefits associated with each objective in a multidimensional way.[137] Thus, there is a movement towards the management theory of "satisficing" and away from the notion of maximizing.[138]

While multiobjective planning is quantitative (it is based on operations research), Cohon's description of its five steps[139] can be the format for a multiobjective analysis with or without quantification:

1. Identify (quantify) objectives.
2. Define decision variables and constraints. Decision variables are the "controls which the decision makers have available to them." Constraints are the limits on those controls.
3. Develop feasible alternatives based on the constraints.
4. Evaluate the alternatives' impacts on the objectives.
5. Select the preferred alternative "through a political selection process."

Cohon claims that it is the multiobjectiveness of the situation that makes a political decision necessary. If the situation involved a single objective, steps 4 and 5 would be combined and quantification would be the decision rule.[140]

Another approach to multiobjective decision analysis is the planning balance sheet (PBS) technique. PBS is similar to CBA because the costs, benefits, and distributional effects are included.[141] Each alternative's effect on all of the objectives is quantified and ranked or weighted. These "scores" are aggregated, and the alternative with the best total score is considered the best. Therefore, Button implies that a political decision is not necessary (other than for providing weights or rankings) and, presumably, the system might still be used as a decision rule.

In any case, multiobjective analysis is the appropriate tool when more than one objective is present and when many of the costs or risks are nonmonetary.

Presentation of Alternatives

In the proposed system, the analysis must present alternative strategies for meeting the regulatory goal. Lave's market regulation framework corresponds to a minimum government role--one option that should be included. The no-risk framework corresponds to the opposite extreme in terms of government involvement. Therefore, it, too, must be presented. These two categories of alternatives are discussed in more detail below.

Market Regulation.[142] This framework assumes that explicit regulation is not needed because risks and societal costs are perfectly accounted for in market-derived prices. Presumably each market participant is capable of choosing among jobs and products by examining them. Those items with undesirable characteristics, such as risk, would be eliminated or have a sufficient amount of compensation associated with them. For example, a job with a higher level of risk would have a higher level of monetary compensation.

Obviously, market regulation has numerous drawbacks as a viable regulatory strategy. Perhaps most unrealistic is the presumption of perfect information among market participants. However, regulations could be designed to work _with_ the market so as to augment the market where it fails. For example, if the market does not provide adequate information to workers or consumers in the respective markets, a labeling requirement would be a market-based regulatory strategy.

No-Risk.[143] No-risk defines an extreme level of regulatory stringency. This framework historically has been used for the regulation of carcinogenic food substances. The Delaney clause amendment to the Food and Drug Act of 1950 calls for all carcinogenic elements to be banned or the level of associated risks to be made safe. At the time this was enacted, few carcinogens had been identified, and their effects were uncertain. Thus, it was reasonable to enact such restrictive standards.

In a way, this is the opposite extreme of market-oriented regulation. It may be appropriate if the problem to be corrected is singularly dangerous, for example, in regulating the disposal of nuclear waste. No-risk levels of regulation should be included in the analysis, especially for situations such as those the Delaney clause addresses (carcinogenic elements in food).

CONCLUSION

The analytical conclusions for the analyses in the proposed system should not be regarded as decision rules. If they are accepted as such, there is a false impression that the decision has been made with perfect scientific objectivity. Value judgements are inherent in any regulatory analysis, whether in choosing alternatives or quantifying the magnitude of various costs, benefits, and risks. When the analyses are seen as presentations of the relevant issues and relative magnitudes, the final decision lies with the policymakers. Therefore, the political nature is clear and accountability is set.

The three frameworks presented should be used as vehicles to communicate information. When the correct framework is used, it is more likely that information of the correct type, _displayed in the most useful manner_, will be available to the decisionmaker. The regulatory system should not attempt to hide political ideologies. These should be transparent. Finally, the system should allow the decisionmaker to have sufficient and correct information.

Connerton and MacCarthy are critical of any regulatory analysis that estimates costs and benefits--even the most informal type of CBA or CEA. More often than not, they claim, the amount of uncertainty in the estimates and assumptions makes CBA meaningless.[144] Furthermore, they feel that any requirement for an economic analysis of costs and benefits inevitably will result in a decision rule based on costs and benefits.[145] While this study has valid points, we believe that if accountability is placed securely with the agency administrators, they will not be able to hide behind any type of decision rule, cost-benefit or otherwise.

Appendix 1

13193

Federal Register
Vol. 46, No. 33
Thursday, February 19, 1981

Presidential Documents

Title 3—

The President

Executive Order 12291 of February 17, 1981

Federal Regulation

By the authority vested in me as President by the Constitution and laws of the United States of America, and in order to reduce the burdens of existing and future regulations, increase agency accountability for regulatory actions, provide for presidential oversight of the regulatory process, minimize duplication and conflict of regulations, and insure well-reasoned regulations, it is hereby ordered as follows:

Section 1. *Definitions.* For the purposes of this Order:

(a) "Regulation" or "rule" means an agency statement of general applicability and future effect designed to implement, interpret, or prescribe law or policy or describing the procedure or practice requirements of an agency, but does not include:

(1) Administrative actions governed by the provisions of Sections 556 and 557 of Title 5 of the United States Code;

(2) Regulations issued with respect to a military or foreign affairs function of the United States; or

(3) Regulations related to agency organization, management, or personnel.

(b) "Major rule" means any regulation that is likely to result in:

(1) An annual effect on the economy of $100 million or more;

(2) A major increase in costs or prices for consumers, individual industries, Federal, State, or local government agencies, or geographic regions; or

(3) Significant adverse effects on competition, employment, investment, productivity, innovation, or on the ability of United States-based enterprises to compete with foreign-based enterprises in domestic or export markets.

(c) "Director" means the Director of the Office of Management and Budget.

(d) "Agency" means any authority of the United States that is an "agency" under 44 U.S.C. 3502(1), excluding those agencies specified in 44 U.S.C. 3502(10).

(e) "Task Force" means the Presidential Task Force on Regulatory Relief.

Sec. 2. *General Requirements.* In promulgating new regulations, reviewing existing regulations, and developing legislative proposals concerning regulation, all agencies, to the extent permitted by law, shall adhere to the following requirements:

(a) Administrative decisions shall be based on adequate information concerning the need for and consequences of proposed government action;

(b) Regulatory action shall not be undertaken unless the potential benefits to society for the regulation outweigh the potential costs to society;

(c) Regulatory objectives shall be chosen to maximize the net benefits to society;

(d) Among alternative approaches to any given regulatory objective, the alternative involving the least net cost to society shall be chosen; and

(e) Agencies shall set regulatory priorities with the aim of maximizing the aggregate net benefits to society, taking into account the condition of the

continued

particular industries affected by regulations, the condition of the national economy, and other regulatory actions contemplated for the future.

Sec. 3. *Regulatory Impact Analysis and Review.*

(a) In order to implement Section 2 of this Order, each agency shall, in connection with every major rule, prepare, and to the extent permitted by law consider, a Regulatory Impact Analysis. Such Analyses may be combined with any Regulatory Flexibility Analyses performed under 5 U.S.C. 603 and 604.

(b) Each agency shall initially determine whether a rule it intends to propose or to issue is a major rule, *provided that,* the Director, subject to the direction of the Task Force, shall have authority, in accordance with Sections 1(b) and 2 of this Order, to prescribe criteria for making such determinations, to order a rule to be treated as a major rule, and to require any set of related rules to be considered together as a major rule.

(c) Except as provided in Section 8 of this Order, agencies shall prepare Regulatory Impact Analyses of major rules and transmit them, along with all notices of proposed rulemaking and all final rules, to the Director as follows:

(1) If no notice of proposed rulemaking is to be published for a proposed major rule that is not an emergency rule, the agency shall prepare only a final Regulatory Impact Analysis, which shall be transmitted, along with the proposed rule, to the Director at least 60 days prior to the publication of the major rule as a final rule;

(2) With respect to all other major rules, the agency shall prepare a preliminary Regulatory Impact Analysis, which shall be transmitted, along with a notice of proposed rulemaking, to the Director at least 60 days prior to the publication of a notice of proposed rulemaking, and a final Regulatory Impact Analysis, which shall be transmitted along with the final rule at least 30 days prior to the publication of the major rule as a final rule;

(3) For all rules other than major rules, agencies shall submit to the Director, at least 10 days prior to publication, every notice of proposed rulemaking and final rule.

(d) To permit each proposed major rule to be analyzed in light of the requirements stated in Section 2 of this Order, each preliminary and final Regulatory Impact Analysis shall contain the following information:

(1) A description of the potential benefits of the rule, including any beneficial effects that cannot be quantified in monetary terms, and the identification of those likely to receive the benefits;

(2) A description of the potential costs of the rule, including any adverse effects that cannot be quantified in monetary terms, and the identification of those likely to bear the costs;

(3) A determination of the potential net benefits of the rule, including an evaluation of effects that cannot be quantified in monetary terms;

(4) A description of alternative approaches that could substantially achieve the same regulatory goal at lower cost, together with an analysis of this potential benefit and costs and a brief explanation of the legal reasons why such alternatives, if proposed, could not be adopted; and

(5) Unless covered by the description required under paragraph (4) of this subsection, an explanation of any legal reasons why the rule cannot be based on the requirements set forth in Section 2 of this Order.

(e) (1) The Director, subject to the direction of the Task Force, which shall resolve any issues raised under this Order or ensure that they are presented to the President, is authorized to review any preliminary or final Regulatory Impact Analysis, notice of proposed rulemaking, or final rule based on the requirements of this Order.

(2) The Director shall be deemed to have concluded review unless the Director advises an agency to the contrary under subsection (f) of this Section:

continued

(A) Within 60 days of a submission under subsection (c)(1) or a submission of a preliminary Regulatory Impact Analysis or notice of proposed rulemaking under subsection (c)(2);

(B) Within 30 days of the submission of a final Regulatory Impact Analysis and a final rule under subsection (c)(2); and

(C) Within 10 days of the submission of a notice of proposed rulemaking or final rule under subsection (c)(3).

(f) (1) Upon the request of the Director, an agency shall consult with the Director concerning the review of a preliminary Regulatory Impact Analysis or notice of proposed rulemaking under this Order, and shall, subject to Section 8(a)(2) of this Order, refrain from publishing its preliminary Regulatory Impact Analysis or notice of proposed rulemaking until such review is concluded.

(2) Upon receiving notice that the Director intends to submit views with respect to any final Regulatory Impact Analysis or final rule, the agency shall, subject to Section 8(a)(2) of this Order, refrain from publishing its final Regulatory Impact Analysis or final rule until the agency has responded to the Director's views, and incorporated those views and the agency's response in the rulemaking file.

(3) Nothing in this subsection shall be construed as displacing the agencies' responsibilities delegated by law.

(g) For every rule for which an agency publishes a notice of proposed rulemaking, the agency shall include in its notice:

(1) A brief statement setting forth the agency's initial determination whether the proposed rule is a major rule, together with the reasons underlying that determination; and

(2) For each proposed major rule, a brief summary of the agency's preliminary Regulatory Impact Analysis.

(h) Agencies shall make their preliminary and final Regulatory Impact Analyses available to the public.

(i) Agencies shall initiate reviews of currently effective rules in accordance with the purposes of this Order, and perform Regulatory Impact Analyses of currently effective major rules. The Director, subject to the direction of the Task Force, may designate currently effective rules for review in accordance with this Order, and establish schedules for reviews and Analyses under this Order.

Sec. 4. *Regulatory Review.* Before approving any final major rule, each agency shall:

(a) Make a determination that the regulation is clearly within the authority delegated by law and consistent with congressional intent, and include in the **Federal Register** at the time of promulgation a memorandum of law supporting that determination.

(b) Make a determination that the factual conclusions upon which the rule is based have substantial support in the agency record, viewed as a whole, with full attention to public comments in general and the comments of persons directly affected by the rule in particular.

Sec. 5. *Regulatory Agendas.*

(a) Each agency shall publish, in October and April of each year, an agenda of proposed regulations that the agency has issued or expects to issue, and currently effective rules that are under agency review pursuant to this Order. These agendas may be incorporated with the agendas published under 5 U.S.C. 602, and must contain at the minimum:

(1) A summary of the nature of each major rule being considered, the objectives and legal basis for the issuance of the rule, and an approximate

continued

schedule for completing action on any major rule for which the agency has issued a notice of proposed rulemaking;

(2) The name and telephone number of a knowledgeable agency official for each item on the agenda; and

(3) A list of existing regulations to be reviewed under the terms of this Order, and a brief discussion of each such regulation.

(b) The Director, subject to the direction of the Task Force, may, to the extent permitted by law:

(1) Require agencies to provide additional information in an agenda; and

(2) Require publication of the agenda in any form.

Sec. 6. *The Task Force and Office of Management and Budget.*

(a) To the extent permitted by law, the Director shall have authority, subject to the direction of the Task Force, to:

(1) Designate any proposed or existing rule as a major rule in accordance with Section 1(b) of this Order;

(2) Prepare and promulgate uniform standards for the identification of major rules and the development of Regulatory Impact Analyses;

(3) Require an agency to obtain and evaluate, in connection with a regulation, any additional relevant data from any appropriate source;

(4) Waive the requirements of Sections 3, 4, or 7 of this Order with respect to any proposed or existing major rule;

(5) Identify duplicative, overlapping and conflicting rules, existing or proposed, and existing or proposed rules that are inconsistent with the policies underlying statutes governing agencies other than the issuing agency or with the purposes of this Order, and, in each such case, require appropriate interagency consultation to minimize or eliminate such duplication, overlap, or conflict;

(6) Develop procedures for estimating the annual benefits and costs of agency regulations, on both an aggregate and economic or industrial sector basis, for purposes of compiling a regulatory budget;

(7) In consultation with interested agencies, prepare for consideration by the President recommendations for changes in the agencies' statutes; and

(8) Monitor agency compliance with the requirements of this Order and advise the President with respect to such compliance.

(b) The Director, subject to the direction of the Task Force, is authorized to establish procedures for the performance of all functions vested in the Director by this Order. The Director shall take appropriate steps to coordinate the implementation of the analysis, transmittal, review, and clearance provisions of this Order with the authorities and requirements provided for or imposed upon the Director and agencies under the Regulatory Flexibility Act, 5 U.S.C. 601 *et seq.*, and the Paperwork Reduction Plan Act of 1980, 44 U.S.C. 3501 *et seq.*

Sec. 7. *Pending Regulations.*

(a) To the extent necessary to permit reconsideration in accordance with this Order, agencies shall, except as provided in Section 8 of this Order, suspend or postpone the effective dates of all major rules that they have promulgated in final form as of the date of this Order, but that have not yet become effective, excluding:

(1) Major rules that cannot legally be postponed or suspended;

(2) Major rules that, for good cause, ought to become effective as final rules without reconsideration. Agencies shall prepare, in accordance with Section 3 of this Order, a final Regulatory Impact Analysis for each major rule that they suspend or postpone.

continued

(b) Agencies shall report to the Director no later than 15 days prior to the effective date of any rule that the agency has promulgated in final form as of the date of this Order, and that has not yet become effective, and that will not be reconsidered under subsection (a) of this Section:

(1) That the rule is excepted from reconsideration under subsection (a), including a brief statement of the legal or other reasons for that determination; or

(2) That the rule is not a major rule.

(c) The Director, subject to the direction of the Task Force, is authorized, to the extent permitted by law, to:

(1) Require reconsideration, in accordance with this Order, of any major rule that an agency has issued in final form as of the date of this Order and that has not become effective; and

(2) Designate a rule that an agency has issued in final form as of the date of this Order and that has not yet become effective as a major rule in accordance with Section 1(b) of this Order.

(d) Agencies may, in accordance with the Administrative Procedure Act and other applicable statutes, permit major rules that they have issued in final form as of the date of this Order, and that have not yet become effective, to take effect as interim rules while they are being reconsidered in accordance with this Order, *provided that,* agencies shall report to the Director, no later than 15 days before any such rule is proposed to take effect as an interim rule, that the rule should appropriately take effect as an interim rule while the rule is under reconsideration.

(e) Except as provided in Section 8 of this Order, agencies shall, to the extent permitted by law, refrain from promulgating as a final rule any proposed major rule that has been published or issued as of the date of this Order until a final Regulatory Impact Analysis, in accordance with Section 3 of this Order, has been prepared for the proposed major rule.

(f) Agencies shall report to the Director, no later than 30 days prior to promulgating as a final rule any proposed rule that the agency has published or issued as of the date of this Order and that has not been considered under the terms of this Order:

(1) That the rule cannot legally be considered in accordance with this Order, together with a brief explanation of the legal reasons barring such consideration; or

(2) That the rule is not a major rule, in which case the agency shall submit to the Director a copy of the proposed rule.

(g) The Director, subject to the direction of the Task Force, is authorized, to the extent permitted by law, to:

(1) Require consideration, in accordance with this Order, of any proposed major rule that the agency has published or issued as of the date of this Order; and

(2) Designate a proposed rule that an agency has published or issued as of the date of this Order, as a major rule in accordance with Section 1(b) of this Order.

(h) The Director shall be deemed to have determined that an agency's report to the Director under subsections (b), (d), or (f) of this Section is consistent with the purposes of this Order, unless the Director advises the agency to the contrary:

(1) Within 15 days of its report, in the case of any report under subsections (b) or (d); or

(2) Within 30 days of its report, in the case of any report under subsection (f).

continued

(i) This Section does not supersede the President's Memorandum of January 29, 1981, entitled "Postponement of Pending Regulations", which shall remain in effect until March 30, 1981.

(j) In complying with this Section, agencies shall comply with all applicable provisions of the Administrative Procedure Act, and with any other procedural requirements made applicable to the agencies by other statutes.

Sec. 8. *Exemptions.*

(a) The procedures prescribed by this Order shall not apply to:

(1) Any regulation that responds to an emergency situation, *provided that*, any such regulation shall be reported to the Director as soon as is practicable, the agency shall publish in the **Federal Register** a statement of the reasons why it is impracticable for the agency to follow the procedures of this Order with respect to such a rule, and the agency shall prepare and transmit as soon as is practicable a Regulatory Impact Analysis of any such major rule; and

(2) Any regulation for which consideration or reconsideration under the terms of this Order would conflict with deadlines imposed by statute or by judicial order, *provided that*, any such regulation shall be reported to the Director together with a brief explanation of the conflict, the agency shall publish in the **Federal Register** a statement of the reasons why it is impracticable for the agency to follow the procedures of this Order with respect to such a rule, and the agency, in consultation with the Director, shall adhere to the requirements of this Order to the extent permitted by statutory or judicial deadlines.

(b) The Director, subject to the direction of the Task Force, may, in accordance with the purposes of this Order, exempt any class or category of regulations from any or all requirements of this Order.

Sec. 9. *Judicial Review.* This Order is intended only to improve the internal management of the Federal government, and is not intended to create any right or benefit, substantive or procedural, enforceable at law by a party against the United States, its agencies, its officers or any person. The determinations made by agencies under Section 4 of this Order, and any Regulatory Impact Analyses for any rule, shall be made part of the whole record of agency action in connection with the rule.

Sec. 10. *Revocations.* Executive Orders No. 12044, as amended, and No. 12174 are revoked.

Ronald Reagan

THE WHITE HOUSE,
February 17, 1981.

[FR Doc. 81-5790
Filed 2-17-81; 3:19 pm]
Billing code 3195-01-M

Appendix 2

A Checklist for DOT Regulatory Evaluations

PROBLEM STATEMENT, ASSUMPTIONS, AND ALTERNATIVES

a. Is the objective properly stated with regard to the real problem?

b. Is a base case explicitly stated and all cost components identified?

c. Are all assumptions reasonable; are they identified and explained?

d. Are assumptions neither too restrictive nor too broad?

e. Are intuitive judgements identified as such? Are uncertainties treated as such? Can the facts be verified?

f. Are all feasible alternatives considered, including those outside the scope of the specific legislative provision?

g. Are the alternatives well defined and discrete? Do they overlap?

COMPARISON OF COSTS AND BENEFITS

a. Does the study indicate why certain costs and benefits were considered relevant and others not? What impacts may have been overlooked?

b. Are the sources of data included? Are those sources valid? Are estimates current and supportable?

c. Are sunk costs and benefits excluded?

d. Are extrapolations adequately justified?

e. Are the parties bearing the costs and reaping the benefits identified? Has any differential time-phasing of costs and benefits been noted?

f. Have external or indirect costs and benefits been included? Are the real resource costs differentiated from financial transfers?

g. Is the arithmetic correct? Were calculations done in constant dollars and discounted?

h. Could benefits be expressed in dollar terms? If not, were cost-effectiveness techniques used? Were all nonmonetary benefits specifically identified?

SELECTING FROM ALTERNATIVES

a. What criteria were used in evaluating alternatives?

b. Have alternatives been ranked according to those criteria?

c. Is the alternative with the greatest net benefits chosen? If not, why did the ranking criterion produce a different result?

d. Are the recommendations logically derived from the material?

e. Is it clear that the proposed action would produce better results than no regulatory change or having no regulation at all?

f. Is overlap from related alternatives avoided?

g. Are the recommendations feasible in the real world of political, cultural, or policy considerations?

h. Are the recommendations based upon significant differences between the alternatives? Have all the variables that might affect the outcome been identified? If necessary, was a sensitivity analysis conducted?

i. Are recommendations intuitively satisfying? If not, can the reasons be identified?

j. Were the methods and sources of the study adequately documented?

APPENDIX 3

HISTORY OF COST-BENEFIT ANALYSIS BY THE FEDERAL GOVERNMENT

The concept of cost-benefit analysis (CBA), broadly defined as the rational weighing of merits and drawbacks associated with the consequences of decisions, has been used ever since man could reason. As a formal tool for decisionmaking, it has been in existence for nearly 150 years. In the spirit of nineteenth century utilitarianism and neoclassical economics, the CBA concept formally appeared first in the writings of Jules Dupuit, a French economist in 1844.[146]

Federal use of CBA began in the 1930s, when the federal government shifted from a laissez-faire spirit to a more interventionist approach. That shift, caused primarily by severe economic hardships, was reinforced by the exigencies of war and firmly entrenched by periods of economic prosperity and rising social and economic expectations.[147]

Beginning with the Flood Control Act of 1936, Congress required the use of CBA for evaluating a variety of public works projects. The United States was in the midst of the Great Depression, and the government was anxious to invest as much as it could without flagrant waste. For example, the Flood Control Act specifically required the government to improve waterways and to install flood control measures provided that "the benefits to whomsoever they may accrue are in excess of the estimated costs" Similar congressional directives accompanied other projects that were intended to resuscitate agriculture in the midwest and in the far west.

The expansion of the use of CBA in the government continued during World War II and the years shortly thereafter. During the War, both the British and American governments recognized the value of these methods to solve well-defined, tactical problems. CBA came to be regarded as one of several public policy research tools, along with other analytical techniques, such as operations research and systems analysis. All of these methods were concerned with the systematic exploration of what might be termed "technical possibilities." "Systematic" implies being orderly and comprehensive in research, fairly explicit in procedures, and quantitative--rather than qualitative--in the mode of measurement.[148]

During the 1940s, the federal government began to standardize its procedures for estimating costs and benefits. In 1946, a Subcommittee on Benefits and Costs was established by the Federal Inter-Agency River Basin Committee to develop common procedures for determining the benefits and costs of water resource projects. In May of 1950, the Subcommittee issued its report, which became known as the "Green Book." This basic handbook included procedures for the measurement of benefits and costs, interest and discount rates, price levels, and risk allowance, and described cost allocation methods for multi-purpose projects.

1950 TO 1970

There were a number of government actions concerning the economic evaluation of water resource projects subsequent to the "Green Book," which further standardized CBA procedures. The Bureau of the Budget (now OMB) issued Circular A-47 in 1952, outlining CBA procedures for use in the Executive Office of the President in reviewing agency reports. The Inter-Agency Committee on Water Resources, late in 1954, established the Subcommittee on Evaluation Standards to succeed the Subcommittee on Benefits and Costs. This group recommended that the "Green Book" be revised. Senate Resolution 148, adopted in January of 1958, also expressed the sense that the procedures for the evaluation of land and water resource projects should be clarified. It directed that certain evaluation information for projects be included in reports. A revised "Green Book" was issued in May of that year.[149]

CBA began to be applied to government programs on a large scale in the 1960s, first in the Department of Defense and then in the emerging Great Society programs for health, education, and welfare. In 1965, the Budget Bureau formally adopted benefit-cost techniques in the form of the Planning Programming Budgeting System (PPBS), a method developed earlier by Defense Secretary Robert McNamara. PPBS included the main elements of CBA: alternative strategies were compared and present and future benefits and costs were specified and measured. The approach was to be uniformly applied throughout the government.

The use of the PPBS procedure was not long sustained by the government, due to several practical reasons. First, the precise application of CBA, including the measurement of all social costs and benefits of government intervention, is impossible.[150] Also, while CBA can identify preferred alternatives among similar program objectives, its ability to evaluate different or immeasurable program objectives is questionable. PPBS seemed to cause unnecessary paperwork and was effectively abandoned a short time later.

RECENT HISTORY

Despite the unsuccessful federal use of cost-benefit techniques, the concept of CBA has continued to receive government attention over recent years. Growing concern over environmental affairs led Congress to pass the National Environmental Policy Act (NEPA), effective January 1, 1970, which required the use of cost-benefit techniques to prepare Environmental Impact Statements (EISs). Specifically, these statements reflected an attempt by Congress to require valuation of environmental resources to consider with economic costs and benefits.[151]

CBA standards were in the forefront again in 1973 in the Water Resources Research Council publication called <u>Establishment of Principles and Standards for Planning--Water and Related Land Resources</u>.[152] These standards permitted agencies to weigh environmental values against the benefit-cost calculation so that a project whose costs were greater than benefits could be approved if the environmental considerations were sufficiently large. In addition, the guidelines candidly concluded that no single calculation could measure the social desirability of a project.

The Nixon Administration sustained federal CBA use by directing the OMB to institute a system of Quality of Life Review. This procedure required all EPA regulations to go through a rather lengthy interagency review process (average review time lasted two years),[153] based on CBA principles. Critics contended that the review process unnecessarily extended the rulemaking process and limited public debate.[154] The Quality of Life review was ended in January 1977 by the Acting Administrator of EPA.

Presidents Ford, Carter, and Reagan implemented regulatory review programs based on CBA. As is clear from the discussion in Chapter 2, Ford's and Carter's are rather broad and general, while the Reagan program calls for specific analysis of costs and benefits and implies that the cost-benefit test should be the deciding factor for the promulgation of new rules and regulations.

NOTES

[1]Nicholas A. Ashford, "The Usefulness of Cost-Benefit Analysis in Decisions Concerning Health, Safety, and the Environment," pp. 2, 3. Unpublished draft based on testimony to various U.S. House of Representatives subcommittees, undated.

[2]For a similar comparison, see also Lawrence J. White, Reforming Regulation: Processes and Problems (Englewood Cliffs, N.J.: Prentice-Hall, Inc., 1981), pp. 29-37.

[3]The Council is composed of all executive branch regulatory agencies plus a number of independent agencies. It is charged with creating a government-wide calendar of forthcoming significant regulatory proposals and actions. The calendar provides a means of examining overall and sectoral regulatory impacts. It is also charged with addressing problems of duplication and conflicts among regulatory agencies (White, Reforming Regulation, pp. 21, 22).

[4]U.S. Regulatory Council, A Survey of Ten Agencies' Experiences with Regulatory Analysis (Washington, D.C.: U.S. Regulatory Council, May 1981), p. 5.

[5]U.S. House of Representatives, Committee on Ways and Means, Tax Aspects of the President's Economic Program, Hearings before the Committee, Statement of Hon. Donald T. Regan, Secretary of the Treasury (Washington, D.C.: Government Printing Office, 1981), 24 February 1981, p. 12.

[6]W.S. Moore, ed., Regulatory Reform: Highlights of a Conference on Government Regulation (Washington, D.C.: American Enterprise Institute, 1970); U.S. Congress, Committee on Interstate and Foreign Commerce, Subcommittee on Oversight and Investigations, Federal Regulation and Regulatory Reform, (Washington, D.C.: Government Printing Office, October 1976); White, Reforming Regulation, p. 19.

[7]Thomas G. Moore, "Transportation," Regulation, January/February 1982, pp. 27-29.

[8]Richard E. Cohen, "Regulatory Report: Federal Policy Shifting in Its View of Economic Regulation," National Journal Reports, 22 February 1975, p. 267.

[9]U.S. Senate, Committee on the Judiciary, The Regulatory Reform Act, Senate Report 97-284, to accompany S 1080, (Washington, D.C.: Government Printing Office, 1981), p. 50.

[10]U.S. General Services Administration, Office of the Federal Register, The United States Government Manual 1981/1982, (Washington, D.C.: Government Printing Office, 1981), p. 45.

[11]U.S. Senate Judiciary Committee, Regulatory Reform Act, pp. 51, 52.

[12]Ibid., pp. 93-95.

[13]Ibid., p. 97.

[14]President's Commission for a National Agenda for the Eighties, Government and the Regulation of Corporate and Individual Decisions in the Eighties (Washington, D.C.: Government Printing Office, 1980), pp. 47, 48; David M. Welborn, "Taking Stock of Regulatory Reform," prepared for the annual meeting of the American Political Science Association, Washington, D.C., 1977, pp. 16-19.

[15]U.S. Senate Judiciary Committee, The Regulatory Reform Act, pp. 96, 97.

[16]"Notes: Regulatory Analyses and Judicial Review of Informal Rulemaking," Yale Law Journal, vol. 91, 1982, pp. 741-743.

[17]"Notes: Regulatory Analysis and Judicial Review," pp. 749, 750.

[18]S 1080 was simultaneously referred to the Judiciary Committee and the Government Operations Committee. Both reported out versions of the bill. The bill that was adopted was a "consensus substitute." (Ibid., p. 750.)

[19]U.S. Senate Judiciary Committee, Regulatory Reform Act, pp.106-175. Section by section analysis of S 1080.

[20]Welborn, "Taking Stock of Regulatory Reform," p. 3.

[21]Christopher DeMuth, "The White House Review Programs," Regulation, January/February 1980, p. 18.

[22]Cass R. Sunstein, "Cost-Benefit Analysis and the Separation of Powers," in "Symposium: Cost-Benefit Analysis and Agency Decision Making: An Analysis of Executive Order No. 12,291," Arizona Law Review, vol. 23, 1981, p. 1280.

[23]"Ford's Inflation Text," Congressional Quarterly Weekly Report, 12 October 1974, pp. 2830, 31.

[24]Executive Order 11821, "Inflation Impact Statements," 39 Federal Register 41502, 29 November 1974,; Executive Order 11949, "Economic Impact Statements," 42 Federal Register 1017, 31 December 1976.

[25]"Notes: Regulatory Analyses and Judicial Review," p. 747.

[26]James C. Miller III, "Lessons of the Economic Impact Statement Program," Regulation, July/August 1977, p. 16.

[27]U.S. Regulatory Council, Survey, p. 1.

[28]Welborn, "Taking Stock of Regulatory Reform," p. 3; Richard E. Cohen, "Regulatory Report: White House Task Force Turns its Sights Toward Congress," National Journal, vol. 7, no. 47, 22 November 1975, pp. 1603-1606.

[29]Miller, "Lessons," pp. 15-18.

[30]U.S. Regulatory Council, Survey, p. 1.

[31]Ibid.

[32]White, Reforming Regulation, p. 19.

[33]Executive Order 12044, "Improving Government Regulations," 43 Federal Register 12661, 24 March 1978; Executive Order 12221, "Improving Government Regulations," 45 Federal Register 44249, 1 July 1980.

[34]Executive Order 12044.

[35]Ibid.

[36]Ibid.

[37]U.S. Regulatory Council, Survey, p. 2.

[38]George Eads, "Harnessing Regulation: The Evolving Role of White House Oversight," Regulation, May/June 1981, p. 21; White, Reforming Regulation, p. 21.

[39]Office of the Press Secretary to the Vice President, "Statement by Vice President George Bush Regarding the Membership and the Charter of the Presidential Task Force on Regulation Relief," January 30, 1981, in Materials on President Reagan's Program of Regulatory Relief, Washington, D.C., 1981, pp. 41, 42.

[40]Ibid., p. 42.

[41]"Excerpts from America's New Beginning: A Program for Economic Recovery, Submitted to Congress by President Reagan on February 18, 1981," in Materials, p. 57.

[42]Executive Order 12291, "Federal Regulation," 46 Federal Register 13193, 17 February 1981, section 1(b).

[43]Ibid., section 6(a)(1).

[44]Ibid., section 6(a)(4).

[45]Ibid., section 6(a)(2).

[46]Ibid., section 6(a)(6).

[47]Ibid., section 3(d).

[48]Ibid., section 8(b).

[49]Ibid., section 3(f)(1) and (2).

[50]"Deregulation HQ: An Interview on the New Executive Order with Murray L. Weidenbaum and James C. Miller," Regulation March/April 1981, p. 18.

[51]Ibid., p. 17.

[52]Executive Order 12291, section 6(a)(6) and section 3(c)

[53]Ibid., section 5.

[54]Ibid., section 4.

[55]Ibid., section 6(a)(5).

[56]The White House, Office of the Press Secretary, "Summary Fact Sheet: The President's Economic Relief Program and Regulatory Relief," 13 June 1981, pp. 4, 5, in _Materials_, pp. xii, xiii.

[57]Office of the Press Secretary to the Vice President, "Statement by the Vice President Regarding Actions Taken by the President's Task Force on Regulatory Relief," 25 March 1981, attachment, "Rules Designated for Postponement," in _Materials_, pp. 73-78.

[58]Ibid., attachments, "Existing Regulations to be Reviewed," in _Materials_, pp. 79-88.

[59]"Statement by the Vice President," in _Materials_, p. 70.

[60]U.S. General Accounting Office, _Report to the Chairman, Committee on Governmental Affairs, United States Senate: Improved Quality, Adequate Resources, and Consistent Oversight Needed If Regulatory Analysis is to Help Control Costs of Regulations_ (Washington, D.C.: General Accounting Office, 2 November 1982), p. 68.

[61]U.S. Office of Management and Budget, "Interim Regulatory Impact Analysis Guidance," 12 June 1981, in _Materials_, pp. 31-35.

[62]Norton Grubb, Dale Whittington, and Michael Humphries, "The Ambiguities of Cost-Benefit Analysis: An Evaluation of Regulatory Impact Analyses Under Executive Order 12291," forthcoming in V. Kerry Smith, ed., _Environmental Policy Under Reagan's Executive Order: The Role of Benefit Cost Analysis_ (Chapel Hill: University of North Carolina Press), pp. 15-17.

[63]U.S. Environmental Protection Agency, "Draft: Guidelines for Performing Regulatory Imapct Analyses," 22 June 1982.

[64]Ann Fisher, "An Overview and Evaluation of EPA's Guidelines for Conducting Regulatory Impact Analyses," paper prepared for the Conference on the Implications of Executive Order 12291 for Environmental Policy, October 1982, Chapel Hill, North Carolina, pp. 3, 4.

[65]U.S. Environmental Protection Agency, "Draft Guidelines," p. 10.

[66]Ibid., pp. 10, 11.

[67]Ibid., pp. 13, 14.

[68]Ibid., pp. 8, 9, 18.

[69]U.S., Department of Transportation, Office of Industry Policy, Office of the Assistant Secretary for Policy and International Affairs, _Guidance for Regulatory Evaluations: A Handbook for DOT Benefit-Cost Analysis_ (Washington, D.C., 15 April 1982).

[70]Ibid., Appendices 3, 4, and 5.

[71]Ibid., p. 1.

[72]Ibid., p. 4.

[73]Ibid., pp. 10, 14, 15, 24-27.

[74]U.S. General Accounting Office, Control Costs, p. 4.

[75]Ibid., p. 50. It is also criticized in Eads, "Harnessing Regulation," p. 21.

[76]U.S. House of Representatives, Committee on Energy and Commerce, Subcommittee on Oversight and Investigations, The Role of OMB in Regulation, hearings before the subcommittee, 18 June 1981, (Washington, D.C.: Government Printing Office, 1981), pp. 53-57, 61-70. (Exchange between subcommittee members and James C. Miller III, Administrator for Information and Regulatory Affairs, Office of Management and Budget and Director, Presidential Task Force on Regulatory Relief.)

[77]U.S. General Accounting Office, Control Costs, pp.48, 49.

[78]U.S. Presidential Task Force on Regulatory Relief, Reagan Administration Achievements in Regulatory Relief; A Progress Report (Washington, D.C., August 1982).

[79]Martin Rosenberg, "Presidential Control of Agency Rulemaking: An Analysis of the Constitutional Issues That May be Raised by Executive Order 12291," in "Symposium: Cost-Benefit Analysis and Agency Decision Making: An Analysis of Executive Order No. 12291," Arizona Law Review, vol. 23, 1981, p. 1205.

[80]Ibid., p. 1221.

[81]Executive Order 12291, section 2.

[82]Rosenberg, "Presidential Control," p. 1202.

[83]Ibid., pp. 1227, 1231.

[84]Paul M. Bangser, "An Inherent Role for Cost-Benefit Analysis in Judicial Review of Agency Decisions: A New Perspective on OSHA Rulemaking," Boston College Environmental Affairs Law Review, vol. 10, September 1982, pp. 374-375., cited by Julius W. Allen, Cost-Benefit Analysis in Federal Regulation: A Review and Analysis of Developments, 1978-1984, Congressional Research Service, Report No. 84-74 E, 15 May 1984, p. 7.

[85]Richard N. L. Andrews, "Cost-Benefit Analysis as Regulatory Reform," in Swartzman, Daniel, Liroff, and Croke, eds., Cost-Benefit Analysis and Environmental Regulations: Politics, Ethics, and Methods (Washington, D.C.: Conservation Foundation, 1982), p. 108., cited by Allen, Cost-Benefit Analysis in Federal Regulation, p. 7.

[86]Robert Sugden and Alan Williams, *The Principles of Practical Cost-Benefit Analysis* (Oxford, Eng.: Oxford University Press, 1978), p. 94.

[87]William C. Apgar and H. James Brown, "Readings for Planning 202" (draft), Department of City and Regional Planning, Harvard University, 1981, p. 538.

[88]U.S. General Accounting Office, *A Technical Guide to Assessing and Preparing Economic Impact Analysis of Regulatory Legislation* (Washington, D.C.: Government Printing Office, 1980), p. 9.

[89]Ibid.

[90]Sugden and Williams, *Principles*, p. 231.

[91]U.S. Office of Management and Budget, "Interim Guidance," in *Materials*, pp. 32, 33.

[92]Edward Gramlich, *Benefit-Cost Analysis of Government Programs* (Englewood Cliffs, N.J.: Prentice-Hall, Inc., 1981), p. 54.

[93]Apgar and Brown, "Readings," p. 577.

[94]Sugden and Williams, *Principles*, p. 134.

[95]Gramlich, *Benefit-Cost Analysis*, pp. 95-107.

[96]Sugden and Williams, *Principles*, pp. 52, 53.

[97]U.S. Office of Management and Budget, "Interim Guidance", in *Materials*, p. 31.

[98]Ibid., pp. 31-35.

[99]U.S. Department of Transportation, National Highway Traffic Safety Administration, Office of Program and Rulemaking Analysis, *Final Regulatory Impact Analysis: Amendment to FMVSS 208, Occupant Crash Protection: Rescission of Automatic Occupant Protection Requirements* (Washington, D.C., October 1981).

[100]U.S. Department of Interior, Bureau of Land Management, *Final Regulatory Impact Analysis for Regulations Affecting Hydrocarbon Operations with the Channel Islands, Point Reyes Farallon Islands National Marine Sanctuaries* (Washington, D.C., January 1982).

[101]U.S. Department of Agriculture, Farmers Home Administration, *Final Regulatory Impact Analysis: Revision of Definition of Low Income for Section 502, 504, and Approved 515 as Required by P.L. 96-153* (Washington, D.C., 14 September 1981), p. 1.

[102]U.S. Department of Interior, *Final Regulatory Impact Analysis of Options to Change the Application Fees and Rental Structures of the Federal Onshore Oil and Gas Leasing Program* (Washington, D.C., January 1982).

[103]U.S. Department of Transportation, Federal Aviation Administration, Office of Aviation Policy and Plans, Final Regulatory Evaluation of Metropolitan Washington Airports Policy (Washington, D.C., October, 1981).

[104]U.S. Office of Management and Budget, "Interim Guidance," in Materials, pp. 33, 34.

[105]Ibid., p. 35.

[106]U.S. Department of Transportation, Rescission of Occupant Protection Requirements, p. XI-13.

[107]U.S. Department of Agriculture, Final Regulatory Impact Analysis, p. 6.

[108]U.S. Department of Transportation, Washington Airports Policy.

[109]U.S. Department of Interior, Federal Onshore Oil and Gas Leasing Program.

[110]U.S. Department of Agriculture, Farmers Home Administration, Final Impact Statement: Proposed Amendments to the Redesignation of Regulations Covering Section 502 Rural Housing Loan Policies, Procedures and Authorizations (Washington, D.C., 3 October 1981).

[111]U.S. Department of Agriculture, Farmers Home Administration, Final Regulatory Impact Analysis: Interest Credit (Subsidy) to Moderate Income Borrowers (Washington, D.C., 3 October 1981).

[112]U.S. Department of Commerce, National Oceanic and Atmospheric Administration, Office of Ocean Mineral and Energy, Final Regulatory Impact Analysis and Final Regulatory Flexibility Analysis for Regulations to Implement Public Law 96-283, The Deep Seabed Hard Minerals Resources Act (Washington, D.C., September 1981).

[113]U.S. Department of Interior, Bureau of Land Management, Final Regulatory Analysis for Regulations Covering Competitive Oil and Gas Leasing in the National Petroleum Reserve in Alaska (Washington, D.C., 30 April 1982).

[114]U.S. Department of Transportation, Rescission of Occupant Protection Requirements, Appendix A, p. 2.

[115]U.S. Department of Transportation, Rescission of Occupant Protection Requirements.

[116]U.S. Department of Labor, Preliminary Regulatory Impact Analysis on Proposed Office of Federal Contract Compliance Regulation (Washington, D.C., undated), p. 12.

[117]U.S. Department of Agriculture, Farmers Home Administration, Final Impact Statement: Establishing New Area-Based Low and Moderate Income Limits for Farmers Home Administration (FmHA) Rural Housing Program (Washington, D.C., 11 December 1981).

[118]U.S. Department of Transportation, Washington Airports Policy.

[119]U.S. Department of Labor, Preliminary Regulatory Impact and Regulatory Flexibility Analysis on Davis-Bacon Related Regulations (Washington, D.C., undated); and Federal Contract Compliance Regulation.

[120]U.S. Department of Transportation, National Highway Traffic Safety Administration, Plans and Programs, Office of Program and Rulemaking Analysis, Final Regulatory Impact Analysis: Part 581 Bumper Standards (Washington, D.C., May 1982), sec. VII, pp. 12, 34.

[121]U.S. Department of Agriculture, Establishing New Income Limits, pp. 10-12.

[122]U.S., Department of Interior, Channel Islands, Point Reyes Farallon Islands, Executive Summary, p. 8.

[123]U.S. Department of Commerce, National Oceanic and Atmospheric Administration, Office of Ocean Mineral and Energy, Ocean Thermal Energy conversion: Final Regulatory Flexibility Analysis (Washington, D.C., July 1981), p. 4.

[124]Ibid., pp. 4, 8.

[125]U.S. Department of Labor, Regulatory Impact Analysis: Suspension of Pension Benefits Upon Reemployment of Retiree (Washington, D.C., undated).

[126]U.S. Department of Labor, Preliminary Regulatory Impact Analysis of Proposed Service Contract Act Regulations (Washington, D.C., undated); Davis-Bacon Related Regulations; and Federal Contract Compliance Regulations.

[127]U.S. Department of Interior, Channel Islands, Point Reyes Farallon Islands.

[128]U.S. Department of Labor, Suspension of Pension Benefits, p. 19.

[129]Ibid., pp. 18, 19.

[130]U.S. Department of Transportation, Bumper Standards, sec. III, p. 80.

[131]Stephen Breyer, Regulation and Its Reform (Cambridge, Mass.: Harvard University Press, 1982), p. 152.

[132]Lester B. Lave, The Strategy of Social Regulations: Decision Frameworks for Policy (Washington, D.C.: Brookings Institution, 1981).

[133]Edward S. Quade, "Introduction and Overview," in Thomas A. Goldman, ed., Cost-Effectiveness Analysis (New York: Frederick A. Praeger, Inc., 1967) p. 2.

[134]Ibid., pp. 4, 5.

[135]Lave, Strategies, pp. 19, 20.

[136]U.S. Environmental Protection Agency, "Guidelines for Performing Regulatory Impact Analysis" (draft), 22 June 1982, p. 18.

[137]Jared L. Cohon, An Assessment of Multiobjective Solution Techniques for River Basis Planning Problems (Cambridge, Mass.: Department of Civil Engineering, Massachusetts Institute of Technology, 1973), p. 76.

[138]K.J. Button, "Models for Decision-Making in the Public Sector," Omega, vol. 7, no. 5, 1979, p. 405, citing H.A. Simon, "Theories of Decision-Making in Economics and Behavioral Science," American Economic Review, vol. 49, 1959, pp. 253-83.

[139]Cohon lists six steps, the sixth being implementation.

[140]Jared L. Cohon, Multiobjective Programming and Planning (New York: Academic Press, 1978), p. 16.

[141]Button, "Models for Decision-Making," p. 406.

[142]Based on Lave, Strategies, pp. 9-11.

[143]Based on Lave, Strategies, pp. 11-13.

[144]Marguerite Connerton and Mark MacCarthy, Cost-Benefit Analysis and Regulation: Expressway to Reform of Blind Alley?, National Policy Papers, no. 4 (Washington, D.C.: National Policy Exchange, 1982), pp. 27, 28.

[145]Ibid., p. 31.

[146]Gramlich, Benefit-Cost Analysis, p. 7.

[147]U.S. Senate, Committee on Government Affairs, Hearings on Regulatory Reform Legislation of 1981, 97th Cong., 1st sess., June 23, 1981, pp. 436-37.

[148]William A. Niskanen, ed., Benefit-Cost and Policy Analysis (Chicago: Aldine Publishing Co., 1972), p. 50.

[149]Inter-Agency Committee on Water Resources, Subcommittee on Evaluation Standards,Proposed Practices for Economic Analysis of River Basin Projects (Washington, D.C.,: Government Printing Office, May 1950).

[150]Gramlich, Benefit-Cost Analysis, p. 8.

[151]S. Fred Singer, Cost-Benefit Analysis as an Aid to Environmental Decision Making (McLean, Va.: Mitre Corporation, 1977), pp. 11, 12.

[152]Robert Dorfman, Forty Years of Cost-Benefit Analysis, Discussion Paper No. 498 (Cambridge, Mass.: Harvard University Press, 1976), pp. 22, 23.

[153]U.S. Congress, Senate Committee on Environmental and Public Works, Subcommittee on Environmental Pollution, Hearings on Executive Branch Review of Environmental Regulations, 96th Cong., 1st sess., 1979, pp. 62, 63.

[154]Ibid., pp. 63-66.